Parenting
Young Athletes
the **RIPKEN WAY**

Also by Cal Ripken, Jr.

THE ONLY WAY I KNOW (with Mike Bryan)

PLAY BASEBALL THE RIPKEN WAY:
THE COMPLETE GUIDE TO THE FUNDAMENTALS
(with Bill Ripken and Larry Burke)

Parenting
Young Athletes
the **RIPKEN WAY:**

Ensuring the Best Experience
for Your Kids in Any Sport

CAL RIPKEN, JR.
with Rick Wolff

**GOTHAM
BOOKS**

GOTHAM BOOKS
Published by Penguin Group (USA) Inc.
375 Hudson Street, New York, New York 10014, U.S.A.
Penguin Group (Canada), 90 Eglinton Avenue East, Suite 700, Toronto, Ontario M4P 2Y3, Canada
(a division of Pearson Penguin Canada Inc.); Penguin Books Ltd, 80 Strand, London WC2R 0RL, England;
Penguin Ireland, 25 St Stephen's Green, Dublin 2, Ireland (a division of Penguin Books Ltd); Penguin
Group (Australia), 250 Camberwell Road, Camberwell, Victoria 3124, Australia (a division of Pearson
Australia Group Pty Ltd); Penguin Books India Pvt Ltd, 11 Community Centre, Panchsheel Park,
New Delhi—110 017, India; Penguin Group (NZ), cnr Airborne and Rosedale Roads, Albany, Auckland
1310, New Zealand (a division of Pearson New Zealand Ltd); Penguin Books (South Africa) (Pty) Ltd,
24 Sturdee Avenue, Rosebank, Johannesburg 2196, South Africa

Penguin Books Ltd, Registered Offices: 80 Strand, London WC2R 0RL, England

Published by Gotham Books, a division of Penguin Group (USA) Inc.

First printing, April 2006
10 9 8 7 6 5 4 3 2 1

Gotham Books and the skyscraper logo are trademarks of Penguin Group (USA) Inc.

LIBRARY OF CONGRESS CATALOGING-IN-PUBLICATION DATA
Ripken, Cal, 1960–
   Parenting young athletes the Ripken way : ensuring the best experience for your kids in any sport / Cal
Ripken, Jr. with Rick Wolff.—1st ed.
   p. cm.
   ISBN 1-59240-219-4 (hardcover)
1. Sports for children.   2. Parenting.   I. Wolff, Rick, 1951–   II. Title.
   GV709.2.R523   2006
   796.083—dc22   2005037752

Printed in the United States of America
Set in ITC New Baskerville with display in Futura
Designed by BTDNYC

This book is dedicated to

Vi Ripken and Cal Ripken, Sr.,

who taught me, my brothers, and sister

what great sports parents, and

great parents overall, really are.

Contents

Contents

Foreword

I was amused when Cal told me that he was approached about writing a book for sports parents. I wondered what qualifies us to speak about this issue. Just like everyone else, we are parents struggling to do what is best for our children.

After some thought and talking to Cal about it, I began to look at the idea of this book a little differently. In today's society, parents need a resource to gain another perspective on this sensitive issue.

Although Cal and I are similar to other parents, his notoriety as a professional athlete puts us in the unique position of witnessing behaviors that others might not see.

As the overprotective mom, the issue that I am most sensitive about is the pressure that is put on my children, Rachel and Ryan, when they compete. They are both good athletes and very successful in the sports they play. However, because they are Cal's children, they face higher expectations from parents, coaches, spectators, teammates, and opponents. This additional pressure is especially true for Ryan because he is Cal's son. It is unfair, and I am always amazed at his resilience and ability to perform under this enormous pressure.

As his parent and protector, I just want him to enjoy the sport he is playing. Children put enough pressure on themselves to succeed. They do not want to be the kid who strikes out, drops the ball, or makes the last out. Our role as Ryan's parents is to protect our child from the additional pressures that others put on him because he is Cal's son. Many people look upon Ryan solely as the son of a great athlete, and they allow no room for error. They expect him to be a flawless athlete. Both Cal and I recognize that the pressure others put on Ryan is unhealthy for him, so we continuously strive to ease that pressure and make all sports a good experience for him.

When we were kids we played sports for fun and exercise. Rarely did a parent or coach look at an eight-, nine-, or ten-year-old child and try to groom him or her into a professional athlete. Over the last two decades, that has changed. As professional athletes became celebrities, with a lot of media exposure and enormous contracts, many parents became excited about any talent exhibited by their child. As parents groomed their children to be the next Cal Ripken, Tiger Woods, or Michael

Jordan, they no longer had the opportunity to enjoy the sport for fun, without the pressures associated with success.

In my opinion—which is a bit jaded when it comes to my children—Rachel and Ryan are the best kids in the world. We are extremely fortunate that both of them have managed to stay grounded despite the attention they receive as Cal's children.

Throughout this book, Cal talks about "returning the games to the kids." I love this phrase, because I believe that this is what needs to happen. When I have the chance to just sit back and watch kids play and interact with one another, there are rarely any problems. The problems usually occur when "grown-ups" get involved.

As a mom, I think it is a natural instinct to be animated and passionate when it comes to my children. Cal and I have learned many valuable lessons from Rachel's and Ryan's athletic events. We continuously strive to make sure that our passion for our children does not override our responsibility to behave and exhibit good sportsmanship for others.

This is an evolving learning process for all of us. Cal and I hope that this book will help you as you continue to grow as a "sports parent." We certainly do not profess to have all the answers but maybe the experiences we have encountered with our children will offer you some guidance.

Being a parent in today's world is tough enough. Being a sports parent presents another set of challenges. If we put our child's needs and dreams ahead of ours, we will have a great chance of "returning the games to the kids."

—Kelly Ripken

Parenting
Young Athletes
the **RIPKEN WAY**

Chapter 1

WELCOME TO SPORTS PARENTING

A very small percentage of kids who participate in youth sports will ever go on to play their sport professionally, but they can all love sports their entire lives.

I just wanted to say that right at the start. If you believe this statement, it will help you make the sporting experience a great one for your child.

Let me ask you a very straightforward question about your child:

What do you want him or her to get out of playing sports?

In the ongoing rush these days to make sure our children are signed up for youth teams, be certain that their practice schedules don't conflict with after-school activities, ensure that we can juggle their game schedules, work out car pools so that the kids can get to practice and then be picked up afterward, and so on, I think that sometimes we don't ask ourselves this very basic question.

The reason I ask it is that a lot of parents come to me as if I have some sort of extraordinary insight or magical formula as to how they can raise their youngsters to become the next Alex Rodriguez or Derek Jeter. I think these parents are always a little disappointed when I tell them that I don't have that kind of inside secret. In fact, the truth is, when I was a kid playing sports, my own parents didn't push activities onto me or my siblings at all. Yes, they were certainly supportive of our athletic activities, but there was no master plan to get us to the big leagues. Now that I think about it, I don't think my dad came to more than one or two of my games when I was in high school, much less when I was playing in the youth leagues.

I can recall when I was nine years old, growing up in Aberdeen, Maryland, and I had just played in a game in which I had pitched and struck out a lot of batters. I remember overhearing a mom of one of the kids from the other team, and she was consoling her son, saying, "That's okay . . . His dad is in professional baseball, and he probably takes his son out all the time and works with him on his game." When I heard this, I looked at my mom with a quizzical expression that said, *Well, that's not true. Dad's not even around.*

The truth was, my dad was usually away coaching in the minors, and it was Mom who came to my games. It wasn't my dad. And when he was around, he had a quiet, gentle patience. He was a teacher of the game of baseball, not a yeller or screamer.

So let me go back to that original question: *What do you want your child to get out of playing sports?*

Let me put this question to you in another way. Deep down inside, do you expect your child to develop into a true athletic star—maybe even someday receive an athletic scholarship to play in college? Or do you feel that your youngster might be good enough to turn pro?

Or maybe you look upon sports in a different way. You hope that your child simply finds that he very much enjoys playing competitive sports (regardless of what that sport may be), and that along the way, he learns about all that sports have to offer—concepts like sportsmanship, team play, competition, commitment, dedication, and sharing in the fun of playing with one's teammates and friends.

That last component of the equation is very important. I've played in a lot of baseball games over the years. When I reflect on all the wonderful times I had playing ball, one of my most important memories is how much I enjoyed the camaraderie, the laughs, and all the fun that my teammates and I shared. In fact, even looking back at the big-league level, that is what I miss most about the game. As a sports parent today, I hope my own kids, sixteen-year-old Rachel and twelve-year-old Ryan, enjoy the same kind of fun times that I did. To me, that's what playing youth sports is truly all about.

I know all too well that many sports parents become too caught up in their children's athletic careers—whether they're good enough to make the local travel team, or if they're going to be named to the league all-star team, or if they're going to be named captain of their team. But to me, that's missing the point.

We all want only the best for our children, but when it comes to sports, you have to first understand the parameters of your child's development. For example, realize that the timeline for her development in organized sports starts around the age of five or six. It's around that age— when children are in kindergarten or preschool—that most communities offer local sign-up registration forms for soccer or T-ball.

At these very tender ages, most children have only the vaguest notion of the sport they're going to play. They just know that (a) they're going to be playing with their friends, (b) they'll be wearing a shiny new uniform, and (c) Mom and Dad will be watching on the sidelines.

Now fast forward to the future for a moment, to your child being a senior varsity athlete in high school. Since, according to the NCAA, only a very small percentage (less than 5 percent) of all high school varsity athletes ever go on to play sports in college (at either the Division I, II, or III level), that means that for most kids, their career in organized sports will come to an end when they graduate from high school. So, in effect, from the time your little one runs off to play in his very *first* game to the very *last* game he plays in high school, he has only about twelve years to be introduced to sports, develop his skills, learn the rules, work hard, and progress all the way to the high school varsity level.

I think you would agree that, in the grand scheme of life, twelve years is a relatively short period of time to go from being a total beginner to being an accomplished varsity player. And during those twelve years, kids are busy doing other things: going to school full-time, doing their homework, developing friendships, and perhaps even working at a job part-time; in other words, they're not just playing sports all day.

Kids explore other aspects of life as they grow up, pass through adolescence, and enter their high school years. Perhaps that's why, according to the Institute of Youth Sports at Michigan State, close to 75 percent of all kids who play organized sports stop playing sports entirely by the time they turn thirteen. To me, that's a very disturbing statistic.

Certainly many youngsters, as they progress through elementary and middle school, find other areas of intrigue and enjoyment, such as the school theater, music, computers, and so forth. That's to be expected as kids seek out and discover their real interests. But I would expect a much larger percentage of kids to keep on playing sports than do. Some sports parenting experts say the high rate of attrition is due to too much pressure being applied to kids early on; that is, if children begin to realize that they are not going to be a true star on their teams, then they begin to wonder whether all their time and effort is really being put to good use.

As parents, we all have expectations for our kids; that's only natural. But in the world of youth sports, we have to be careful not to lay our expectations on our children. If we somehow suggest to our kids that if they advance in sports, then they will make us proud, we're setting our kids (and ourselves) up for disappointment. In other words, instead of the twelve-year-old child saying to herself, *Gee, playing sports is a lot of fun and I love it,* she ends up asking herself, *Why should I bother to keep playing sports when it's clear that I'm never going to live up to Dad's expectations? After all, I'm not going to be the captain of the team, or make the all-star team, so why should I keep playing?*

It's that kind of question that too many of our kids are asking themselves at too young an age, and from my perspective, it shows how our priorities have shifted. *Yes, playing sports is still supposed to be about having fun.* But I worry whether we, as adults, have drifted too far from that basic premise in the hope that our children will be the chosen ones who grow up to become the next Michael Jordan or Mia Hamm.

IT'S STILL ABOUT HAVING FUN

In the Ripken household, Kelly and I have tried very hard to keep fun as the major attraction of sports for Rachel and Ryan. Kelly and I believe that very young kids should be exposed to a variety of sports when they're just starting out, so that they can pick and choose for themselves what they want to pursue. In Rachel's case, she has played a number of sports, including field hockey and lacrosse, but in high school, she has been drawn primarily to dancing and basketball. There was no pushing or prodding. Kelly and I firmly believe that kids have to have their own inner motivation to drive them in competitive sports. That is, Rachel dances and plays hoops simply because they're fun things to do. That's great. And we hope that as Rachel goes on with her life, she will continue to play sports, dance, and exercise so that she stays physically fit and healthy.

Ryan, too, was exposed to a variety of sports when he was very young. But over the years, he has found himself increasingly attracted to baseball, basketball, and soccer. He hasn't specialized in any one sport yet, and he plays all of his sports with a real competitive spirit. It's clear from the way he approaches his games that he has an inner drive to push himself to become better and improve athletically.

Did either Kelly or I push Ryan in this direction? Absolutely not. He's just a kid. And we believe that kids today—just like when we were growing up—find their own way in sports. When I was a youngster in Maryland, my brothers, Billy and Fred, and I played everything from bowling to basketball to soccer to baseball to football. We played them all because they were fun, we loved to compete, and we were kids! It was only after getting to the high school level that I began to focus more on baseball, but even when I was in high school, I still continued to play soccer and basketball recreationally. Heck, I still play basketball today!

Mom certainly didn't push us. She was very supportive and interested in how we were doing in sports, but she wasn't watching over the coach's shoulder, nor was she analyzing how our games were developing. Mom encouraged us because she knew that sports were healthy outlets for her kids and that we looked forward to them.

Dad was a minor league coach and manager during my youth baseball years. He was coaching in Elmira, Rochester, Dallas, and so on. He was early to report in spring training, gone all spring and summer, and then in the instructional league in the fall. He didn't get home to Baltimore until November. We would join him for a week or two in spring training, and then after school in July and August, but otherwise, he really wasn't drilling us in the backyard. We just played our games and had fun.

WHY I BECAME INVOLVED IN SPORTS PARENTING

Kelly and I became interested in sports parenting as soon as we had our kids. Like you, we take tremendous pride in our children, just as our parents did in us when we were growing up. Yes, our adult lives are very full and busy, but our children come first. For many years, Rachel and Ryan have been involved in athletics, and we want to be there for them, to share in their fun and make certain that they enjoy the ride.

Chances are you have the same sentiments. We all know that time goes by very quickly, and, as noted above, when it comes to sports, the clock starts ticking very early in our kids' lives. We all acknowledge and accept that. But regardless of how far your child pursues his sporting career, the one basic question you want to ask yourself along the way is: *Did my child enjoy himself?*

In fact, people always ask me how I determine whether a youngster has had a good season. I know that they're asking me whether, from a statistical perspective, I think their child did well. But to me, a "good season" is better defined by whether the athlete had so much fun that she wants to sign up and play again next year. As a sports parent or youth coach, that should be your overriding criterion as to what kind of season your child had. Remember, three out of four kids quit by the time they're thirteen!

With Ripken Baseball, I make this our mission. We're not trying to make big-league players out of the kids who play; rather, we're simply trying to give them a sense of enjoyment, and of sportsmanship, and of how to develop and be better at their individual baseball skills. We're trying to teach baseball concepts and give them a much greater appreciation of the game.

When I speak at the kids' banquet during our World Series, which is held each summer in August, I always point out that: "There's only going to be one winner who comes out of this tournament . . . but this tournament really isn't about crowning a champion. This is all about having a positive life experience. Just because your team doesn't win doesn't mean that this will not be fun for you. Enjoy it all and compete fairly, and make friends with kids from other teams and other countries. Sports should be a *life* experience for kids—not a winning or losing experience."

HOW TO USE THIS BOOK

This book was designed to help guide you through the increasingly complicated world of sports parenting. It's based upon all of my experiences—as a young athlete, as a professional athlete, and as a sports parent myself. I've tried to touch upon most of the common experiences that sports parents go through with their kids, starting from the youngsters' first introduction to sports, and continuing up to the time they reach middle school. As such, this book is organized chronologically, with the emphasis first being on the preschool years, then the elementary school years, and finishing with the middle school years. The chapters provide a road map for you as your young athletes progress and grow through these stages.

It's important to understand and acknowledge that sports in the twenty-first century is much different than when we were kids. That is, what worked for us as kids twenty or thirty years ago may not have any application for our children today. It's a different world. When we were growing up, there were a lot fewer distractions. For example, routine household entertainment that all of our children take for granted—such as computers, video games, the Internet, skateboards, cable TV, instant messaging, and so on—weren't even dreamed of when we were growing up.

Coaching philosophies are also different. When we were developing, most coaches were traditionally stern taskmasters whose rules and regulations were never to be broken or challenged. Some coaches wouldn't even allow kids to get a drink of water during football practices on hot August afternoons. I can even recall that, back in the day, most baseball coaches openly frowned on ballplayers doing any weight training, claiming that such activities would only hurt a ballplayer's arm or back. In short, times have changed. And this book will help you guide your children through their paces in today's sports. Along the way, I've provided some sample scripts, dialogues, and sports-parenting techniques that I believe may be of help to you.

CAUTION—CHILDREN AT PLAY!

As sports parents, we have all heard the horror stories about parents who try to live their own dreams vicariously through their children. Psychologists tell me that it's hard to pinpoint why today's parents do this, but they do say that this trend is clearly much more prevalent with modern sports parents than it was with our moms and dads.

Perhaps sports parents now feel that their child is that special one—the one-in-a-million youngster who will develop into the next great professional superstar. And to help ensure that their youngster fulfills her destiny, these parents start to plan and design her athletic career from day one. That may mean getting her to play on more than one team during a crowded season, perhaps getting her signed up for private instruction during the week, or maybe even sending her to specialized sports camps in the summer. While none of this is, of itself, a bad or wrong move, what is essential here is that it's the youngster who is driving this—not a parent who is attempting to relive his or her childhood dreams. That's important to understand and recognize. *The drive has to come from the child—not you.*

In my travels and talks, it's amazing how many sports parents will tell me about their kids who play ball or other sports and how excited they are about their children's success. And I must admit that sometimes I fear that the proud parent is already convinced that his or her nine-year-old is on the fast track to become an athletic superstar, and that the parent is doing everything to make absolutely certain that the child's sports career will go a lot further than the parent's own.

I try to caution parents: Remember, that little guy or gal out on the field is indeed your flesh and blood, but is *not* you. That little one is her own person, who comes complete with her own hopes, dreams, and aspirations in sports and in life. So be very careful about putting your own lost or dashed dreams onto hers. The bottom line is that your childhood is over: It's done, finished, and it's in the books. And your child's life experiences in sports are going to be her own, no matter what.

The best way to ensure that your youngster will enjoy his youth sports experience is to be supportive and positive, and above all, let him have some fun. The advice in this book is all based upon that simple philosophy. It's what I believe in.

Key Chapter Takeaways

1. **Ask yourself: Is your child truly having fun playing youth sports? That is, does he look forward to going to the games and practices? Does he have a smile on his face when he plays?**

2. **As a sports parent, do you fully accept that your childhood is over . . . and that your child has dreams of her own when it comes to sports?**

3. **Have realistic dreams for your child, and above all, be careful to avoid putting too much pressure on him. In the long run, sports are more about kids staying healthy and physically fit, and simply enjoying the experience.**

Chapter 2

THE PRESCHOOL YEARS

Try to think back all the way to when you were a four-year-old.

If you can, try to remember what your first introduction to sports was like.

Maybe someone gave you a football helmet for Christmas one year and you ran around all day with that helmet on, pretending you were a rough-and-tough NFL star. Or maybe you can recall watching a figure skating competition on television, and you fell in love with the artistry, grace, music, and exciting drama of all the jumps and moves on the ice. Or perhaps you can recall going to your first baseball game at a major league ballpark, what it was like to walk down the ramp in the mezzanine, and your first glimpse of that shiny emerald green field down below.

Or, on the other hand, maybe you never had a particularly great experience with sports when you were a kid, and you want to turn things around for your children.

Regardless of your background in sports, if you want to become the best sports parent you can be, then read on!

Regardless of what sport you fell in love with, it's a good bet that your lifelong love affair with sports started with that first spark of passion. A passion to drink in and play that sport to your fullest. For many of us, falling in love with sports was just a natural part of our childhood. I know that when I was growing up, my brothers, Billy and Fred, and I were always playing one sport or another. We were attracted to, and loved, the thrill of athletic competition. Bowling leagues. Ping-Pong tournaments. Touch and sometimes tackle football on the sandlots. Basketball, soccer, and of course baseball. We played all day, with breaks only for lunch and for dinner. And with our kids today, that's still where it all starts—with that instinctive passion to play. Kids still fall in love with sports at a very early age.

But the truth is, without that baseline desire, it makes no difference whether your kid is extraordinarily gifted. No youngster goes on to become a star in anything in life unless she has that internal drive, that inner motivation, that passion to perform. So how does one fan the flames of that passion for a youngster? In my opinion, when your child is four or five, all you want to do is to introduce him or her to a variety of sports. You simply *expose* your child to different sports at this early age. Let her see which sports she likes and looks forward to. Encourage him to experiment a bit. And don't be concerned if she jumps from one sport to another when she is this young. That's what kids do. Give them a chance to try a bunch of sports.

Just let your child kick a soccer ball. Or dribble a basketball. Or have a catch with her in the backyard. Allow your child to watch sporting events on television with you. Or take him to a real high school, college, or pro game. If your child asks questions (and don't worry, she will), have the patience to answer them. If you don't know the answers, ask a friend or consult a basic handbook on the sport.

I have wonderfully fond memories of watching minor league ballplayers in action when my dad was coaching and managing in the minors. In particular, Billy and I would pick out our favorite players, and then try to copy their individual batting styles and other mannerisms. We did this for years, and we loved it. These days, lots of young ballplayers have private coaches that they work with. Imitating the minor leaguers we saw play was our version of private coaching.

By the way, don't be discouraged if your little one's attention span is very short during these very young years. Kids are like that. They'll play catch for just a few minutes, only to want to run after a butterfly they've spotted in the yard, or to pet the family dog. Or they'll want to run inside and watch a favorite show on television.

All of this is normal. Accept it. What you don't want to do is to *force* your child to go out and practice his sport with you. Nothing will turn your child away faster from athletics than if you order, or demand, that he keep practicing. Remember, at age four or five, it's all just *child's play*. Once you start making it mandatory, the play quickly transforms into *child's work*—and once play turns into work, you will have quashed your child's passion.

I write this because I know there are some serious sports parents who believe that the sooner you can get your youngster on the right path in sports, the sooner she can get a leg up on the competition. But by age four or five? That just doesn't make any sense. Long before your youngster can even start thinking about becoming a serious competitor, she first has to develop that passion. Being told to go out and practice and practice some more just doesn't work for any kid.

Once I had a parent tell me that he treats baseball and homework in the same way. Every day after school his son has to do two hours of homework and two hours of baseball practice. I asked how old the child was and was told he was seven! Then I asked the parent how his son reacted to this tough regimen. The parent told me that his boy didn't like it very much, but that someday he would definitely thank him. I believe the opposite will occur. The first time the parent isn't there, standing over the child, the boy will choose to do something else, as the game will have long before stopped being seen as fun, but rather as a chore.

THE MYTH OF TIGER WOODS'S CHILDHOOD

But what about the great golfer Tiger Woods? Wasn't he a child prodigy playing his game when he was only three? And didn't Tiger's dad push him hard every day to improve his game?

Yes, Tiger was a child prodigy. At age three, he was driving a ball off a tee in a very impressive manner. That's just a rare quirk of early athletic talent, and it occasionally happens. But that other notion, about his father pushing him every day, is actually a myth. According to Earl Woods, who, by the way, was a pretty decent college baseball player at Kansas State University, he was thrilled by Tiger's potential. But being a former athlete himself, Earl was smart enough to know not to push his son. In fact, according to Earl's own accounts on how he raised Tiger, every day when school was over he would routinely ask his son whether he wanted to go out and hit some golf balls. Most of the time, Tiger eagerly went along. But on some days, Tiger told his dad no, that he wanted to go off with his friends and do the kinds of things that young kids do. Whenever Earl heard that from his son, he gladly put the golf balls and clubs away for the day. Earl knew instinctively that once you make practice mandatory for a youngster, the child's play will transform into laborious—and unwanted—work.

New Trends in Kids' Leisure Time

According a study by the Kaiser Family Foundation and the Centers for Disease Control, on any typical day kids today are six times more likely to play a video game than to ride a bike.

As recently as 1995, more than two-thirds of all American kids who were ages seven to ten rode a bike at least six times a year. Fewer than half rode a bike last year, as sales of two-wheelers dropped from 12.4 million in 2000 to 9.8 million in 2004.

Instead, eight- to ten-year-old kids are now playing video games, or are on the computer, an average of six hours a day! And that number goes even higher during the summer.

Ryan loves his video games, and I don't try to make him give up those games, because he enjoys them so much, and that wouldn't be fair. I do, however, on occasion give him a choice between playing video games indoors or playing with me outdoors, and he always picks me. I would encourage all parents to try to incorporate some outdoor activity with their children whenever they can.

KIDS DEVELOP IN SPORTS AT THEIR OWN SPEED

Let me relate another story about how kids develop at their own pace in sports. When Michael Jordan was a sophomore in high school in North Carolina, not only was he not the star of his high school basketball team, he didn't even make the starting five. In fact, Jordan didn't even make the varsity team!

He was fifteen years old at the time, and by all accounts, Michael was just another teenage basketball player with some potential. But he wasn't good enough to make his high school team. After being cut, he went to the varsity coach and asked him what he needed to work on to make the team the following season, when he would be a junior. Michael loved playing basketball; even after being cut, his passion was still there. And to his credit, Michael took the coach's comments to heart, worked his tail off, and the next year he made the varsity. It also helped, of course, that Michael went through a growth spurt and added a few inches in height.

But there are a few important lessons to be learned from Michael Jordan's story. One, he followed his lifelong passion for the game of basketball. He never lost that, even when he was disappointed that he was cut from the varsity. Two, instead of being bitter and just complaining about being cut, he channeled his frustration into making his game even better. That's the kind of internal drive I'm talking about. Adversity is a major part of all sports, and Michael was one of those athletes who was able to transform his adversity into a positive force. That's a theme— overcoming adversity—that I come back to throughout this book. It's my belief that kids have to learn how to deal with setbacks if they are ultimately going to succeed not just in sports, but in life in general. Three, the fact that he grew a few inches underlines the reality that kids will grow and develop according to their own genetic blueprint. The truth is, some kids grow early in their preteen years, and some grow later on.

Case in point. When I was a freshman in high school, I stood about five feet, seven inches tall and weighed just under 130 pounds. Yes, I was a good athlete, but I was far from being the biggest kid in my grade. When I graduated from high school and was drafted by the Orioles, I had grown to six-two, and 180. But by the time I reached the majors, I had grown to six-four, and played at 220 pounds. My growth spurt, like Michael Jordan's, occurred in my later teenage years. That's a not uncommon occurrence for a lot of aspiring athletes.

My point is that neither Michael Jordan nor myself ultimately fell behind the other athletes simply because we either were relatively average size as fifteen-year-olds or because our athletic abilities hadn't blossomed yet. Please keep these examples in mind, because when your child is very young, it's more about her developing that passion for the game than you worrying about how she compares with the other twelve-year-olds or fourteen-year-olds. Again, kids go through growth spurts at different times.

Keep in mind that the opposite takes place as well. Very often the physically imposing twelve-year-old will dominate a sport simply because he matured physically more quickly than other kids his age. His athletic dominance could easily drop off as the other kids go through their own growth spurts.

BUT WON'T MY CHILD FALL BEHIND THE OTHER YOUNG ATHLETES?

No. You have to understand that all kids develop at their own rates. Some kids will grow to their adult size by the time they're twelve. Other kids won't shoot up until they're sixteen or seventeen. Some kids even continue to grow until they're twenty-one. Furthermore, some youngsters will exhibit great flashes of athletic coordination at a very young age, whereas other kids take more time to gradually grow into their bodies. As a parent, this could be somewhat distressing to you, but sometimes, you have to take a step back and reflect on situations as any objective adult would. Again, kids do grow and mature at different rates. We all know that and understand that. But as parents, when we're talking about our own children, it's often very difficult for us to separate our emotions from our intellectual instincts. This is perhaps one reason so many sports parents become so agitated and upset on the sidelines when watching their children in a game. Even though moms and dads all know intellectually that "it's just a kids' game," many parents have a very difficult time keeping their emotions in check when their child is competing on the field.

I mention the innate differences in the ways kids develop because there seems to be a growing anxiety among parents that their athletic youngsters have to keep up with all the other kids in their grade in school. I'm not sure where or how this kind of "keeping up" mentality started, but clearly sports parents start tracking and comparing their children with the other same-age kids at a very early age.

Is this healthy? Of course not. I think you can draw a direct correlation between this mentality and the heightened emphasis on winning that now pervades our youth sports. It seems that what should be our top priority—our kids having fun and enjoying themselves—has somehow taken a backseat to winning, and unfortunately our kids are paying the price.

There are so many factors that go into a child's athletic development (innate talent, passion, drive, the influence of the adolescent years, etc.), that it's pretty much impossible to look at today's six-year-old and determine that she is going to be a star at eighteen. So while there's nothing wrong with feeling a sense of parental pride when your little one scores a goal in a soccer game, or gets a base hit in a T-ball game, let's be a little patient before deciding which sports agent your child is going to sign with.

I'd also caution you about comparing your child's abilities with those of other kids. Remember, there will be plenty of time down the road to figure out just how talented your youngster is. But in order to get to that point, in the beginning years, it's essential that your child go out and have fun playing sports. That's the key—to make sure he has so much fun that he wants to come back next season and play again.

Just a side note. I know that in some communities, travel teams for sports like soccer, hockey, and baseball start having tryouts for kids as young as eight or nine. In effect, this is the first time that your youngster will be compared and evaluated alongside other kids her age. Travel team tryouts can be extremely nerve-racking for everyone involved, and as a sports parent, you have to be fully informed of who's running the tryout and what's expected of your child. Then, talk to your child ahead of time about what will be happening. Give your youngster an idea of how the tryout is going to be conducted, how long it will last, and so on. A little preparation will go a long way here.

I mentioned early on that Ryan played travel baseball for the first time last summer, and I have more to say about travel sports throughout the book. But I will add this one note. My son Ryan, who is now twelve, didn't participate on any full-blown travel teams until he was eleven. When he was younger, Kelly and I felt that he shouldn't be traveling. We wanted him to have a normal, regular kid's life, with lots of time off, sleepovers, birthday parties, and the like. Now that Ryan does play on a travel baseball team, he seems to have a great passion for it because the experience is all so new and exciting for him.

Match the Athlete with His or Her Sports Background

A. MICHAEL JORDAN

1. Played only basketball in college at Arizona

B. LARRY WALKER

2. Was only five-foot-eleven as a senior in high school

C. KENNY LOFTON

3. Got cut from his high school hoops team

D. CYNTHIA COOPER

4. Wanted to be a pro hockey goalie but got cut

E. SCOTTIE PIPPEN

5. Didn't start playing ball until fourteen

F. SAMMY SOSA

6. Didn't start playing ball until sixteen

G. MARK McGWIRE

7. Outstanding goalkeeper in soccer

H. HAKEEM OLAJUWON

8. Was a top college basketball player at UCLA

I. MARK BUEHRLE

9. Not recruited out of high school

J. JOHN STOCKTON

10. Got cut his first two years in high school

K. JACKIE JOYNER-KERSEE

11. Eyesight as a child was 20/500

ANSWERS: A-3; B-4; C-1; D-6; E-2; F-5; G-11; H-7; I-10; J-9; K-8

THE IMPORTANCE OF THE THREE Ps—
PRAISE, PATIENCE, AND PASSION

I once heard someone in youth coaching talk about the three "Ps" when it comes to working with kids, and it made a lot of sense to me. As I recall, in order to ensure that their youngster was on the right track in sports, parents were advised to keep the three Ps in mind: **Praise, Patience, and Passion.**

Passion you already know about. That's the inner drive that fuels your child's love for sports and competition, and his desire to keep going. But in order to keep that passion going, you first need to provide your little one with lots of praise and patience.

Praise is absolutely essential. Children of all ages (and even parents!) respond to good, solid praise. And with a five-year-old who is just trying to learn how to ride a bicycle or swing a bat or throw a spiral with a football, it's your responsibility to praise every effort she makes. It's actually a fairly straightforward cause-and-effect relationship. When your kid hears from you that he's making progress with his athletic skill, or that you are pleased with his efforts, then he will make every attempt to go back and try it again and again. So long as you are sincere and quick with your kind words, then your child will be eager to continue her attempts to master her athletic skill.

Your words of praise should be precise and to the point. *But be careful not to make promises that may not happen.* Here's an example of what I mean:

> SIX-YEAR-OLD: Here, Dad, watch me take a few swings with my bat . . .
>
> DAD: Wow! Mike, that's terrific! You keep that up and next spring the Little League folks in town will be insisting that you play up a level with the older kids!

While the father's words of praise are solid, he has introduced a possibility to his six-year-old that is not under his control. Why make that kind of promise? Perhaps the dad is so eager to see his son progress faster to a higher stage that he feels that he's doing the right thing. But in reality, all he has done is place a level of expectation on his young son that he may not be able to reach. Suppose the six-year-old plays Little League ball next year and is not asked to play up a level? What does the father say to the boy then? Does the boy feel he let his dad down? The bottom line? By using praise in the wrong way, the father may have set his son up for an early disappointment.

Perhaps a better approach would have been:

> DAD: Wow! Mike, that's terrific! You're making great strides as a young hitter. Keep up the good work, because your swing is clearly getting better and stronger.

Mike is still being praised by his dad. And Mike will feel confident that he's making solid progress with his batting stroke. But there's no unnecessary pressure being applied here. Just the good, positive observation from the father to his son that his swing is getting better and better every day.

But what do you say or do when you child falters a bit in her progress? What do you say to your son if he's playing goalkeeper in soccer and he lets a number of goals in? What do you say to your daughter if she drops a pop-up and also lets a grounder go through her legs?

Again, with kids who are just starting out in sports, you have to keep in mind that there are going to be a lot more failures and frustrations than successes. No kid goes out and learns how to ride a bike on her very first try. No youngster plays youth ball and makes every play in the field during his first year. It just doesn't happen because sports aren't that easy.

As kids get older, you will want to give them more feedback on their game, good and bad, as soon as they are through competing for the day. It is important to hold back on any suggestions until the time is right and the emotion from the game has passed.

When your little one comes running off the field to you after getting a taste of the downside of the game, you have to be supportive. And you have to be careful about the words you use. For example, telling a seven-year-old, "Don't worry about making those errors . . . after all, it's just a game" is not going to make that youngster feel any better. In fact, for a young athlete who desperately wants to do well, telling her that "it's just a game" is almost a form of insult. Why? Because in her small and uncomplicated world, that baseball game may be the most important thing in her young life!

Instead, try to choose words of support and praise that ease her pain. Try something like, "I know you would have preferred to have made those plays in the field, but errors are going to happen . . . But what I really liked about you today is that you didn't give up. You kept working hard out there, and you kept giving it your all. That's important and that's what counts."

By the way, don't be surprised if your little one bursts into tears after a tough game. That's not only understandable for a child under ten, it's almost commonplace. If he does start to cry, whatever you do, do not make fun of his tears! Just accept it. This is the time to give your child a solid hug, to give him some brief words of support he wants to hear, and then let him talk about his next activity for the day.

The good news is that for most little ones, the pain and disappointment of a tough day at the ballpark or on the soccer field or basketball court don't last very long. Kids are amazingly resilient, and they don't let their sadness linger too long. Within minutes of their tough outing, the tears will have dried up and they'll be ready to go get a snack or go to a friend's house for a playdate.

When I was twelve, my team came within one win of advancing to the Little League World Series. I pitched in the big game and gave up the home run to lose the game. We were all devastated . . . that is, until our coach took us all fishing about an hour later. It's great to be a kid!

After praise, all sports parents need to have a strong sense of **patience**. Indeed, praise and patience go hand in hand when working with kids. Because they are not going to master difficult athletic skills overnight, it's incumbent on you to be patient, patient, and even more patient. Kids need time—lots of it—to learn the skills of sports, plus they have to learn these skills and master them while their bodies continue to grow and change. And while they're learning these skills, they're going to rely upon you for that daily dose of praise (to let them know that they're on the right path) as well as a solid show of patience as they try, try, and try again to learn how to dribble a basketball with either hand, or how to hit line drives instead of pop-ups. If you don't give them the patience they need, then kids will run the risk of just getting frustrated. When they become frustrated, there's a good chance that they will walk away from that sport. That's precisely why praise and patience are so vital in their development.

When it comes to sports, young kids learn pretty much through trial and error. That's just the way we learned. They have to learn on their own and at their own pace that if they hit a ball on the bat handle on a cold spring day, they're going to feel their hands sting. They have to learn that if they dribble a basketball with only their right hand, then a defender in a game will be able to slap the ball away. In short, they have to find out that the kids who tend to progress in sports are the ones who go out and practice their game a lot. As they get older, they'll find out on their own that if they want to get more playing time in the games, practicing their skills makes them more competitive.

As a parent, you want to help your child any way you can. It shouldn't be a burden on you to praise her efforts in her early years of sports development. Mastering athletic skills should not be overlooked or taken for granted. Kids need to know that they're making progress in their skills, and the very first person they look to is you—their mom or dad—to make sure that you're paying attention, and that they're on the right track. So when they're able to skate on ice for their very first time without your assistance, or they're able to swim across the pool without your help, or they're able to ride their bike without training wheels, this is the perfect time to applaud their athletic accomplishments.

But along the way—when they're going through spills on the ice, or depending on those training wheels, or sputtering in the pool with their inflatable swimmies around their arms—this is an even more important time to be there with a supportive smile and lots of praise for their efforts. Your young child needs your encouragement and patience to get to that next level. You also reassure him constantly so that he will have the inner confidence to master that skill.

Are these early years important? Absolutely. Because these are the first steps down the path of athletic involvement, and kids really need that first shot of self-confidence, parental encouragement, and sincere support to want to keep on progressing. Remember, for all of us, there was a time way back when our own parents helped us get over those first few hurdles. And in the grand scheme of sports, it's a pretty simple formula:

Accomplishment + Self-Confidence =
More Accomplishment + More Self-Confidence

During these early years, you are going to want to jump in right away and show your youngster the right way to swing a bat, or to shoot a basketball, or to swing a golf club. Problem is, despite your best intentions to get your kid on the correct path right away, the vast majority of children who are four or five or six are going to be more interested in doing things their own way. They're just not interested yet in learning the right way.

That's fine. There's nothing wrong with allowing your son or daughter to experiment and to explore all the different ways of swinging a bat or dribbling a basketball. There's also nothing wrong with you occasionally showing him or her how to grip the bat or how to shoot a basketball.

TEACHING THE BASICS THE RIGHT WAY:
THE "PRAISE SANDWICH"

Let me share with you another communication tool I picked up somewhere along the way. I call it the "praise sandwich," but no matter what you call it, it seems to make a lot of sense.

But what happens when my child is now seven and it's clear that she definitely needs some instruction? How does a parent give constructive criticism?

Try giving your child a praise sandwich. This is a very effective device that takes only a few seconds, but can be very powerful in terms of its positive impact on your young athlete. Let me give you an illustration:

Suppose you're watching a group of six-year-olds playing in a soccer game, and your child is dribbling the ball up and down the field, never looking to pass the ball to a teammate. After a while, it's pretty clear your Sam isn't going to share the ball with anyone. The game finally ends and you might be tempted to get back in the family car and address the issue head-on: *C'mon, Sam, what were you doing out there? Why were you such a ball hog? Why didn't you pass the ball to your teammates during the game?*

Imagine what kind of impact those sharp comments would have on Sam. How will Sam play in next week's game, knowing that he might be opening himself to serious criticism if he doesn't pass the ball? Even more, do you think he's going to be eager to go out and practice his dribbling this week, knowing the harsh criticism he just received?

Wait until later that night, maybe after dinner or in a quiet time before bed. Then suppose you said, *Sam, I have to tell you how great you were today in the soccer game. It's clear that your ability to dribble a soccer ball is really coming along very well. And let me tell you something else . . . If you ever get to the point where you not only dribble the ball as well as you do, but can also develop your passing skills to find an open teammate in front of the net . . . well, Sam, there will be no stopping you on the soccer field. If you can develop both of those skills, you'll be on your way to becoming a dynamic soccer player.*

That entire interaction took about thirty seconds. But the positive impact it has on Sam is long lasting and substantial. Not only will he come away knowing that he impressed his parent today with his soccer play, but also that his mom or dad is giving him the guidance on how to take his game to the next level by simply developing his ability to pass the ball! Please note that there are no promises here (e.g., promises of making the all-star team, or of scoring more goals), but there is the promise that if Sam works hard on his skills, then his game will benefit.

Basically, this is the praise sandwich. It's called that because it consists of one slice of simple but honest praise (that's to first get your child's attention—remember, kids immediately perk up when someone is praising them), then there's a center slice of delicately worded constructive criticism (that's the instruction you want to get across), and then it's all wrapped up with another slice of solid praise.

Please do choose your words carefully, especially when it comes to constructive criticism. If you take a few moments and think about the words you want to use *before* you say them, you can transform any criticism you may have of your child's game into a positive approach. That's key. Kids do not respond well to straightforward or blunt criticism. Especially when they are young and still developing their passion for sports, they need to hear as much positive feedback as possible.

All this talk of praise sandwiches really makes me hungry. No, I mean curious. You should know that this is not the kind of terminology I grew up with, so I immediately feel the need to go on a search to find out where this was applicable in my life. As you know, I grew up around minor league baseball, witnessing my dad develop many groups of young men who were trying to get to the big leagues.

Dad believed that true teaching and instruction didn't occur during the heat of a game. The game was for a different type of learning—that is, experiencing the moment. So Dad used to make notes on the game chart for future reference. The pitcher who was to pitch tomorrow's game had the responsibility of keeping the chart. To do this, he was forced to watch the pitch selection and the results of those pitches. As you can tell, there was a simple logic to this process, but Dad took it one step further. He used this process to help identify "teaching moments."

For example, if there was a mistake in the game, he simply asked the pitcher to put a little red dot next to that pitch on the game chart. After the game was over, Dad would go over the chart pitch by pitch to check for accuracy and to relive and identify those teaching moments. When he found one, he simply pulled out an index card and wrote down the player's name and the mistake that was made. Dad would usually pile about ten cards on his desk from a typical game. Then we could go home.

Upon arriving at the park the next day, Dad quickly got dressed in his uniform and waited for the players to arrive. When one of the players who was on his cards showed up, Dad would call him into his office. He would always start off the conversation with a positive comment, something like *You've really been playing well at second base—I love the way you are turning the tough double play.* Then Dad would say, *Hey, sit down and let me go over a little mistake from last night's game.* He might say to Doug DeCinces (one of Baltimore's top players for many years): *Doug, you got thrown out at third base last night in a situation where that can really never happen. We were down two runs late in the game and the heart of the order was coming up. You made the last out at third base and you left our cleanup hitter in the on-deck circle.*

Doug then would offer his explanation for attempting third, and then Dad would always finish on a positive comment, like *Of course there is a time to be more aggressive and a time to be careful, but I want you to know that I love watching you grow as a base runner. You've got great instincts and I want you to tap into them by continuing to be daring and aggressive. Doug, go on out there and get on base another three times tonight.*

The players always walked out of Dad's office with a little extra bounce in their step, but also a little wiser than before they stopped by. Now this whole interaction probably took two minutes, tops, and this is at the pro level. This was Dad's "praise sandwich" technique, and it worked wonders. As you can see, if you can think these lessons through, you'll be able to make a better point faster—and with kids that's a necessity.

Along those lines, understand that as kids get a little older their thirst for praise will never end. They're still going to want to hear praise, praise, and more praise as they go through the elementary, middle, and high school years as well. John Wooden, the great and legendary basketball coach at UCLA, learned early on in his career that he would have to give at least four or five parts praise to every one part criticism to his players. Just criticizing the players on the team, he discovered, did no good; after a while, they just wouldn't listen to him. He found that the more he praised them, the more they would respond to him. And on those occasions when he had to offer some criticism, they were much more open to his comments. Remember, kids, too, respond to praise!

Coaches who only criticize their athletes during the games find out very quickly that their kids will begin to tune them out. Just like good ol' Charlie Brown, who finds his teacher talks only in white noise, kids who have a coach who keeps on yakking during the game just tune the coach out!

WHAT'S THE RIGHT SPORT (OR SPORTS) FOR YOUR CHILD?

That's hard to say. You really have no idea which sports your youngster will gravitate to until she has been exposed to a bunch of them. When he's five or six, the best way to get a sense of what your child would like to play is to show him as many sports as you can. Your youngster may know about football from watching it on television, or baseball from going to the youth league games in town, or basketball, or skateboarding, or cheerleading—you name it. When the registration forms come in the mail, you can simply ask whether your child would like to sign up for each sport.

Of course, you may run into a situation where your child wants to play *every* sport. That can be difficult in terms of logistics, time, and expense. Before you run out and purchase all sorts of brand-new football equipment, you might want to let your son borrow some equipment first and then let him go to a few practices to see if he really wants to play football. I recall a mom telling me about her son, who was very gung-ho to play youth league football. But on the first day of practice, when he was carrying the ball and was tackled by the defense, he quickly decided that he disliked the actual physical contact of football and asked if he could play soccer instead.

Kids will do that. They will change their minds about which sports they want to play. As parents, this doesn't make our lives any easier. But remember, when we were kids, no one forced us to make a decision about which sports we were going to play until we were probably entering high school. If that was the case for us, why are we so determined to make our kids choose a sport for life when they're six or seven?

In other words, let your youngster seek out as many sports as she is drawn to. No one ever forced me to make a decision on what the right sport was for me to play. As I got to high school age, I was ultimately drawn more to baseball, but that decision came from me, not from my parents or any of my coaches.

WHAT IF YOUR CHILD PLAYS A SPORT YOU KNOW NOTHING ABOUT?

It does happen. Kids today have much different interests than when you and I were growing up. Just look at how popular the X Games are on television. Kids love to skateboard, snowboard, mountain bike, and do all sorts of athletic events that weren't even invented when I was a kid. Thanks to Lance Armstrong's amazing success in the Tour de France, kids are more aware of the fun of riding bikes competitively, something most of us didn't know about.

As a consequence, you just don't know what sport or sports your child is going to be drawn to. If he does happen to choose a sport that you aren't familiar with, don't be too concerned. Let's assume, for example, that your favorite sport is football, and that you played football ever since you were a kid and right through high school, and that you still continue to play touch football on the weekends and even follow your favorite NFL team religiously. But your six-year-old only talks about Freddy Adu or Mia Hamm and can't wait to practice corner kicks and penalty shots.

The problem is, you know very little about soccer. So what do you do? Do you encourage your child to play football instead? No. Just start educating yourself about soccer. Go to the local library and pick up some instructional books and tapes on how to play the game. Learn about its history, and about its top stars today. In other words, support your child's interests. Rather than discourage your child and try and push him away from a sport that he loves, act like a grown-up and learn to love that sport as well.

WHAT YOUR CHILD REALLY WANTS FROM YOU

In the early developmental years, kids want nothing more than to know that Mom and Dad are watching them and their efforts. When they go outside and want to show off to you how well they can kick a soccer ball or swing a bat or how fast they are when they sprint, they need your undivided attention. They don't want to see you chatting with a neighbor, or watching a pro game on television, or watering the lawn. They want your undivided attention as they go through their attempts at mastering and perfecting their athletic skills.

And in addition to your undivided attention, they also want to hear your supportive praise for a job well done. They want to know that you openly approve of their efforts, that you are proud of what they have accomplished so far. In short, your child wants you to know that she is developing her skills in sport, and in these early years, a lot of her drive to do well has to do with her inherent desire for parental approval. That is what your presence brings to your child.

Criticism and hard-core instruction can wait for a few years. Early on, you just want to make sure your child truly "has fun" while learning about sports. Light his passion and keep it lit.

Key Chapter Takeaways

1. **In their early years, let your kids find and develop their own interests in sports. Don't worry—they will. Just be careful not to push them into only those sports that you like!**
2. **If your child is drawn to a sport you aren't familiar with, take the time to educate yourself about it.**
3. **Learn about the praise sandwich—and then use it. It works!**

Chapter 3

THE ELEMENTARY SCHOOL YEARS (AGES 6–11)

Once your youngster has shown a desire to continue with sports into her elementary school years, there are a few steps to keep in mind as you guide her along her way. Unlike when I was growing up, when youth sports leagues were few and far between and we played only a handful of organized games, today it's the rare community or town where there aren't several organized youth leagues offering a variety of different sports.

As a parent, your responsibility is to educate yourself about the various recreational leagues in your town that your son or daughter may be drawn to. Find out as much as you can about these leagues. Most youth leagues are run by parents who volunteer their time, and usually they have lots of printed information available, or perhaps they even have a Web site.

You don't have to do exhaustive research, but you

should know most of the basics. Find out the following information:

1. When is registration time? Mark the dates on your calendar.
2. How much does it cost to have your child play? Most youth sports programs charge about $50 to $75 for a child to participate.
3. How long does the season last? See if there is a schedule of game and practice dates.
4. Where are the practices and games? Better make sure you know where the fields are located.
5. Who are the coaches in the league? Is the league run by parents who volunteer to coach?
6. What are the league rules about playing time? Bear in mind that in most youth leagues, every child on the team is guaranteed to play in at least half of each game.
7. How are the teams selected? Do the coaches preselect the teams, or does the league hold tryouts so that the teams are chosen equally?
8. What about equipment? Better find out what kinds of running shoes, mouth guards, etc., your child will need to play.
9. Does your child need medical clearance? If your child has a special medical condition, or even if he doesn't, does the league need a pediatrician to sign a clearance paper for your child?

If this is your first time with a child signing up for a youth league, it's most definitely worth your while to find out as much information as you can.

MEETING THE COACH

For most kids, a youth league is the very first opportunity to play for a coach other than their mom or dad. Unless you happen to be serving as either the head or assistant coach on the team, keep in mind that playing for another adult is a new experience for a child. Like meeting one's teacher in kindergarten or first grade, it can be a daunting transition.

Even with Ryan and Rachel, although I have helped out as a head coach or assistant coach on some of their youth teams, I have always felt it was important for them to grow a little bit, in a certain way, away from Kelly and me. Learning how to play for different coaches other than one's parent is an important part of the process.

Your job is to reassure your child that they are going to be in fine hands, that *Coach Smith is a wonderful coach, and you're going to love playing for him.* In other words, do your best to quickly erase any concerns or fears that your little one may have. Most youth coaches will have a mandatory meeting with all the parents to go over their coaching philosophy and to outline all of the details of the upcoming season. The coach may go over the league or team rules regarding playing time for each child, rules about missing practices or games, how important winning is to the coach,

perhaps even some rules from the coach about parental behavior on the sidelines, and so on. If you have any questions
at all, this is the time to bring them up. Chances are that a
lot of the other moms and dads on the team have the same
questions, so you're doing everyone a favor by asking.

Coaches may also say at this time that they're looking
for some parental assistance in terms of serving as a team
parent. A team parent usually makes sure all the kids are
contacted in case a game or practice is rained out or post-
poned. In addition, a team parent usually handles a good
chunk of the other administrative chores, including making sure all the uniforms are handed out, directions are
distributed, and any other minor details that may come up
during the season. When the coach is finished giving the
presentation, be sure to go up to him or her and introduce yourself, and point out which little one is your child.

If there are any other special concerns for your child,
such as medical or psychological needs (e.g., inhalers, dia-
betes, other medications, etc.), this is the right time to
speak with the coach. You may want to have this conversation privately. Be sure to reassure the coach that your son
or daughter is definitely healthy and fit to play, and that
you will be there to help out at all times. Remember, most
coaches at the youth league level are volunteers. They are
not medical professionals, and you should never assume
that they have any training in that area.

You should also assume that most volunteers have little, if any, background in working with kids. That's not a

criticism, but I would love to see volunteer coaches get some training from the league each year. Let's face it, for better or worse, the coaches will have a tremendous influence on the kids, so we all hope that they are sensitive to the kids' individual needs. Fred Engh, the author of *Why Johnny Hates Sports,* has pointed out to me that coaches often have more of a lasting influence on kids than their teachers do.

Unfortunately, it seems that these days our culture is more focused on who's the star than on just getting kids to play up to their potential. Today's coaches and parents have to be very careful about this expectation. If you feel that your kid has to be the star or else playing is not worthwhile, well, then there are going to be some problems. The coach's job is to help each kid develop and get better individually, but also to do this in the context of the team. The coach has to tap into each kid's needs, and then understand what kind of contribution the kid can make to the entire team. At least to me, that is the ideal goal.

LISTEN TO YOUR CHILD

As your six- or seven-year old goes through her first few practices, there will be a great deal of excitement. For most kids, finding out which team they're on, discovering which of their friends are on that team, getting their shiny new uniform, and putting on their new equipment is a very cool thing! Plus they now report to a coaching staff and they now have real games to look forward to!

As a parent, you merely have to stand back and observe their fun. You might want to get to practice a little early, before pickup time, and see how your son or daughter is fitting in with the rest of the kids on the team. You can just watch quietly from the car or from the sidelines. I used to stick around and watch quietly from under a tree. I wanted to observe everything that was going on. Try and get a sense of how your child is doing, and whether he's enjoying himself. Then when practice is over and he bounces back into the car, you can ask him how practice went, how the coach is, when the first game is, and so forth. Most importantly, *let your child do the talking*. Don't be in so much of a hurry to lecture her—let her tell you about what she did.

AVOIDING THE PGA—
THE POSTGAME ANALYSIS

Letting your child do most of the talking is actually going to be an important lesson for you as your child goes through his youth sports experience. Too many moms and dads can't wait to get their children into the family SUV right after the game is over, only to start immediately lecturing them on what they did wrong in the game.

This is known as the PGA—*the Postgame Analysis*. I guess that well-meaning sports parents must figure that the very best time to go over what their youngster did right or wrong in a game is when the contest is still very fresh in their child's mind. They must think that if you wait too long, then the child will forget what she did, and have a much greater chance of repeating those mistakes in the next game.

In reality, the absolute worst time to do a critique of your child is just after the game is over. When he hops back into the car, he is still excited from the game's action, perhaps a bit tired, maybe a bit dirty, maybe frustrated that his team lost, but above everything else, he just wants to hear how well he played! He's eager to hear that you were at the game and saw him do well. Remember, we're talking about kids under the age of ten here, so they're looking strictly for an enthusiastic response from you. This is not the time to give them a full-blown and detailed analysis.

Even better, when you do give your child that positive feedback, try to point to one or two plays in the game where he really shone. *John, remember in the second quarter of the game when you made that simply great pass to Mike? Tell me about that . . .* Or *Sue, that was a spectacular catch you made in center field. How did you do that?*

Remember this: Kids *love* talking about the great plays they made. And when you ask about those plays, they can't stop talking about their big moment. In other words, focus your support and praise on those plays in the game in which they did well. Let them enjoy those moments.

There will be a better time to critique their performance and help teach them when the emotions of the game have passed. But when the game has just ended, dwell on the positives that they can take from the game.

At all costs, stay away from telling them that they have to work on their throwing more, or keep their eye on the ball, or learn how to get a better jump on the ball. While these observations may be valid ones, it's just not the right time to bring them up. In short, if your kid got up four times in a game and struck out three times, but got a hit on the fourth at-bat, this is the time to focus on that hit. You can worry about the three strikeouts at a later time. Right now, let's just celebrate the positive!

By the way, silence is not a bad choice either. Don't ever feel compelled to discuss the game. A period of quiet time on the ride home is fine. Again, take your cues from your child: Let your youngster set the tone.

GO OUT AND HAVE FUN!

Let me back up for a moment. One of the reasons you have to be so careful about avoiding the PGA is because of what you told your child *before* the game began.

Let me ask you this: What's the very last thing we tell our kids when they bound out of the car and run to their game? For most moms and dads, our last line is usually something like *Go out and have fun!*

This is significant. After all, we don't say, *Go out, but you better play well . . . because when the game is over, I'm going to give you a detailed performance appraisal.*

That's essential to keep in mind because kids *do* want to just go out and have fun, and they sure don't expect to get a report card of how well they did that day. And in truth, it takes a little courage and common sense from you, their parent, to give them the space and freedom to go out and do just that. Let your eight-year-old be an eight-year-old!

Giving kids some freedom also means that as they learn sports, they're definitely going to make errors, strike out, forget how many outs there are, walk too many batters, throw to the wrong base, and so on. That's what little kids do when they learn sports. They make mistakes, and they make plenty of them. In time, they will learn from those mistakes. So accept this: In today's game, they will not play flawlessly. Even more important, you should never expect them to. Playing sports is a constant challenge to try to improve. No one, especially a little one just starting out, ever plays a perfect game.

OH NO! MY SIX-YEAR-OLD IS A DAISY PICKER!

You may have noticed that when kids are six or seven, they have relatively short attention spans. And that affects their sports as well. Suppose your kid is playing T-ball and the coach puts her in right field. It's a warm spring day, there's not much action happening with the batter, and before you know it, your child in the outfield is bored. She's looking around at an airplane passing way up in the sky, or perhaps she hears the chimes of the ice cream truck in the parking lot. Whatever the distraction is, she's clearly not into the T-ball game.

And then, of course, a ball is suddenly hit to her in the outfield, and she's picking daisies rather than paying attention to the game at hand. What, as a parent, do you do?

First off, relax. Little kids do occasionally become bored. Try to think back to when you were a kid. You probably got bored in games as well, and your mind also wandered. Back then, if you were daydreaming during a sandlot pickup game, with the exception of your playground friends, nobody cared that you were picking daisies. But these days, we don't give our kids that kind of space or freedom. We expect them to be sharp, fully attentive, and into each pitch. Take it from me—this is just not going to happen.

Don't worry. As your child gets a little older, around eleven or twelve, and becomes more competitive, he'll automatically become more involved in paying attention to the action. That's just the natural progression of his growth in sports.

BACK WHEN I WAS A KID . . .

It wouldn't hurt for you, as the parent, to occasionally mention to your child that when you played ball as a kid, you also had plenty of days when you struck out, when grounders went through your legs, or when you gave up a key home run. Let your child know that you are human, too, and that you had some tough days at the ballpark. This kind of open and honest admission will help your youngster to relax, and will lessen the pressure on her.

We sometimes forget that kids literally and figuratively look up to us, and when we are giving them instructions and tips on how to put a bunt down, or how to toe the rubber properly, or how to make a pivot, we sometimes come across as having mastered all of these skills when we were their age. Please make it clear that all of these athletic skills take years to develop, and that they are just starting out. Let them know that it took you years as well to polish and hone your abilities, and even then, there were days in high school when you made errors or struck out.

THE ESSENTIAL ROLE OF THE ASSISTANT COACH

The coach may also ask for a couple of assistant coaches. Assistant coaches are volunteers who help run the practice sessions and help out on game days, and can run the team in case the head coach can't make it to a practice or game.

I urge you to strongly consider helping out as an assistant coach on your child's team. There are several advantages to doing this. First, it allows you to "officially" be at the team's practices and on the sidelines at the games, whereas all the other parents are restricted to the stands or away from the practice field. Second, while you don't have the full responsibility of being the head coach, being an assistant allows you to move around the children on the team and get to know them and praise them. Third, being an assistant allows you to see up close and firsthand how your child is doing. And fourth, because you are an assistant, you will have a direct line of communication with the head coach on any number of issues that may pop up during the course of a season.

As an assistant coach, bear in mind that other parents who have concerns might feel very sheepish about approaching the head coach. But they'll see you as a filter or buffer, and they will eagerly come to you with their concerns, testing the water before discussing the matter directly with the head coach. For example, a parent might come up to you right after a practice session and ask, *Say, my son was wondering when he might get a chance to pitch on the team? Do you and the head coach have an idea when he might do that?* Or a mom might approach you and ask, *I don't want to bother the head coach with this, but I was wondering . . . We're going away on a family trip in a couple of weeks, and I just wanted to know the protocol if my child misses the game on that Saturday.*

In other words, if you serve as an assistant coach, the other parents of kids on the team will automatically see you as a friend or colleague whom they can approach. Especially if the parents aren't sure of the team policy—then they will definitely come to you first for a clarification. Of course, if you don't have the answer, then you can go to the head coach and act as a go-between.

In this day and age, when too many sports parents lose their perspective when it comes to their kids' athletic careers, the role of the assistant coach has become very important. There's nothing wrong with serving as a buffer, especially if you can do some preventive maintenance so that the lines of communication remain open and strong between parents and coaches. Indeed, most sports parenting experts will tell you that many of the ugly incidents that occur today in youth sports have their roots in a lack of basic communication between the coaching staff and the parents.

IF YOU DECIDE TO SERVE AS AN ASSISTANT COACH . . .

Serving as an assistant coach is a terrific opportunity. But before you volunteer your services, do yourself and your family a favor first by asking your child whether he would like you to be on the coaching staff of his team.

Now, nine times out of ten, your child will be elated and thrilled that her mom or dad is going to be helping out on her youth team. She will immediately break into a smile and think this is the greatest news in the world! But after the celebration dies down a bit, just take a moment to remind your child that, as an assistant coach on the team, you will be treating all of the kids on the team in the same way: *fairly and objectively*. This concept should be introduced to your child as soon as possible, so that there's no misunderstanding on practice day when your six-year-old expects that, because you're one of the coaches, he will be named team captain or will have his choice of whatever position he wants to play.

And if you serve as the head coach of a youth team, again, this entire process should be reviewed with your child. Ask her first if she would like you to be the team's head coach, and then if she says yes, remind her of the rules of equality that you have to enforce as the head coach. By the way, if, for some reason, your child asks that you not be on the coaching staff, either as the head coach or as an assistant—and this does sometimes happen—then you should definitely honor your child's request (remember, this is about his childhood, not yours). But you can certainly ask your youngster why he prefers that you not serve as a coach. In truth, he may not be able to articulate his reasons, but either way, you should ask just once and then honor your child's feelings.

Why would a kid not want her mom or dad to help out? Maybe the youngster already feels the pressure of parental expectation being applied to her. Playing for a different grown-up appeals to her greatly because it means, quite frankly, getting away from the pressures that you may be putting on her. Kids may be young, but they aren't stupid. Even at the earliest ages of youth sports a youngster might feel that Dad is putting too much pressure on him to be a star, and, gee, wouldn't it be great to play for someone else who wouldn't always criticize him or evaluate his play?

The bottom line? If your six- or seven-year old is telling you that she doesn't want you as her coach, think about what she is saying to you. Maybe you ought to take a step back and ask yourself if you're already pushing your child too much in sports. Indeed, maybe the best solution of all is for your child to play for someone else. That way, your child can relax and enjoy playing sports, and you can take a breather as well and give some space to your child.

What Kids Really Want from Their Coach

Sports Illustrated for Kids magazine conducted an online poll at sikids.com. They received one thousand responses from boys and girls, grades K–12. Here are the highlights of what the kids wanted in their ideal coach:

95 percent said that the number-one quality in a coach is the ability to help the players improve their athletic skills.

64 percent said that they would rather play on a losing team for a coach whom they liked than to play for a winning team with a coach whom they didn't like.

62 percent of the kids said that they wanted equal playing time for all the kids on the team. As one twelve-year-old wisely observed, "Everybody should play the same amount so that everybody has the same amount of fun."

61 percent commented that it was okay for the coach to yell during the game—but only if the yelling was of a positive

(continued)

What Kids Really Want from Their Coach

nature. Yelling out instructions to a player is fine, but yelling at a player because she made a mistake humiliates the kid and only makes her feel bad.

93 percent of the kids said that they wanted and needed the coach's full support, regardless of the kid's athletic ability. Wrote one eleven-year-old: "If the coach isn't confident in you, how can you be confident in yourself?"

SO, SHOULD YOU COACH YOUR CHILD?

It's a question that just about every sports parent considers at one time or another, and in my opinion, coaching your child is certainly fine. The possible benefits outweigh the negatives, so long as you maintain a commonsense and balanced approach to your child's needs and the needs of the other kids on the team.

For example, I've talked about being sure to treat all the kids on the team equally and fairly. That's very important. I know some coaches will actually treat the other kids on the team all in one manner, but then will make the practice sessions much tougher for their own child (e.g., *Okay, kids, let's everyone run two laps to get warmed up for practice, but Emily, I want you to be sure to run three laps.*) Coach, you can't do that. It's not fair to the kids on the team, and it certainly isn't fair to your daughter Emily.

And it's not always a physical demand, such as having one's child run more laps or do more drills or more sprints at the end of practice. Sometimes, it's an unfair responsibility. (*Sam, make sure all of the other kids on the team start hustling more throughout the game. They need to do that.*)

Again, it's not fair to ask your son Sam to make sure that all the kids are running more during the game. That's putting responsibility on your son that, quite honestly, he doesn't need and didn't ask for. And it's also not treating either him or the rest of the kids on the team fairly and equally. After all, who appointed your son to be the de facto captain of the team?

Are these little issues? In the grand scheme of life, perhaps they are. Yet I can't tell you how many parents I meet today who are in their thirties, forties, or fifties who vividly recall their youth league baseball or basketball coach and the positive (or negative) impact that coach had on their young lives. Very few of today's sports parents can accurately recall the score of a game from when they were in third grade, but they sure do remember how the coach treated them and their teammates. The game details tend to fade away over time, but the memories of a coach, either good or bad, last for decades. Please keep that responsibility in mind when you're coaching kids.

By the way, if you end up coaching your kid's team, here's a tip to keep in mind: It's always a good idea to have three coaches working with the team. Why? Because each kid will get more individualized attention during the skill and drill practice sessions, which is precisely what the children want. In addition, your child will be exposed to different styles of coaching. Plus, there have been times with my own children when I wanted to say something to them about their game, but I found it much more productive to have one of the other team coaches talk to Ryan or Rachel. You may have already noticed that kids will sometimes listen more carefully to what another grown-up has to say than to their own parent. The same principle applies to sports as well.

BEING A COACH SHOULDN'T CARRY ANY EXPECTATION OF PERKS OR ENTITLEMENT

The kids expect they'll be treated equally, and so do the parents. And when you played sports, you certainly expected it as well. That means that the rules are the same for everyone, and that no one gets special or preferential treatment (especially the son or daughter of the coach). Being a volunteer means that you're giving your time freely and without any expectations. More to the point, being a volunteer coach does not mean that, in consideration of your efforts, you or your child are entitled to special benefits or perks of the job.

Here's what I mean, and admittedly, some of these "perks" range from frivolous to more serious. But if you're going to be a coach, then you have to be sensitive to what impact you're having not just on the kids, but also on their parents, who are watching for any signs of entitlement!

For example, being a coach does not entitle your child to have her choice of what uniform number she wants to wear. (By the way, I always tell Ryan that it doesn't really make much difference what uniform number he gets. I explain to him that while I happened to wear number 8 for a long time with the Orioles, I had all sorts of different numbers when I played in the minors and in high school. I try to point out that it's not so much the uniform number that the player wears but the player inside the uniform that counts.) Being a coach also doesn't entitle your child to be named as a team captain for the season, or to go out for every coin flip at the start of the game. Being a coach doesn't entitle your child to be automatically named to the all-star team. It doesn't entitle your child to be the first in line for every practice drill, or entitle him to get more drill practice than the other kids on the team. Being a coach doesn't entitle you to have your child always serve as a model for the other kids on the team (e.g., *Jon, why don't you show the other kids what I mean by taking a good lead off first base?*)

Your child is not always entitled to bat third and play shortstop, or always play center forward, or be the point guard, or be the quarterback, or play any of the other highly desirable positions on the field. Even if it's true that your daughter is, in fact, the most talented kid on the team, that does not mean you have the right to give her more playing time at the so-called better positions than the other kids.

I can hear some of you coaches saying, *But if we don't play the better kids at the key positions, aren't we jeopardizing our chances to win the game? Is that fair to the rest of the kids on the team and to their parents, who want to see the team win?*

A couple of thoughts on that. **Remember, we're talking about kids under the age of twelve here**. While the kids certainly want to win, at this young age winning is not the top priority. In fact, as far as the kids on the team are concerned, their top priority is more about getting into the game and having a chance to play shortstop or be the point guard or be the quarterback. They all want that chance to show what they can do. *They just want to play!*

And as far as their parents are concerned, whether you want to believe it or not, they come to the games, first and foremost, to watch their kids play—and play a lot. Whether the team wins or not is really a secondary concern to them. They just want to see their little one go out, do his best, and have fun. The parents really couldn't care less about your youth team's won-lost record. In fact, probably the only people who do care about that won-lost record is you and the rest of the coaching staff, and maybe one or two parents on the sidelines.

I trust you get the idea. To be an effective and fair coach, you have to be sensitive to all these issues. The sad truth these days is that most of the other parents on the sidelines will automatically assume that if you're the coach, then you're playing favorites with your son or daughter. Go out of your way to show those parents that you will not abuse your position.

A colleague of mine told me how he handled this issue of entitlement when he coached. When his ten-year-old son played youth league baseball, this coach knew that his boy was one of the better players on the team. But he also knew that if he let him bat third and start at shortstop on Opening Day, all the parents of the other kids on the team would be in the stands clucking their tongues about entitlement.

So the coach pulled all the kids together before the game and explained to them that there were fourteen kids on the team, but only ten could be in the lineup at one time. That meant that four kids would have to sit out the first part of the game, but under league rules, those four youngsters would definitely play in the second half of the game. He then announced the starting lineup for Opening Day, and much to his son's surprise, he was one of the four kids who would be on the bench.

"But, Dad, it's Opening Day! Everybody will be there, watching the game," protested the coach's son. "This isn't fair. I'm one of the best players on the team!" But the coach/father then explained to his son that yes, "you're definitely one of the better players on the team, but the league rules stipulate that somebody has to sit out the first half of the game. And today, along with three other kids, it's your turn to sit first. But don't worry, you'll get in the game later on. I promise you that."

The youngster wasn't happy with this explanation, of course, but the coach/father also knew that his starting lineup (without his son) would send a strong and clear message to all the parents in the stands—specifically that, as the coach, he didn't intend to play favorites, even if it meant having his own son sit out of the starting lineup on Opening Day.

As you might imagine, this message did go out loud and clear to all the parents, and it was greeted enthusiastically. Meanwhile, the coach's son got into the Opening Day game later, played well, and continued to play well during the rest of the season. More importantly, neither the coach's son nor any other player on the team ever complained when it came his time to sit out a few innings. The issue of parental coaching entitlement never came up during the season, because the coach had set the right tone very early on.

Curt Schilling's Favorite Baseball Manager

Hard-throwing right-hander Curt Schilling has pitched in the big leagues for close to twenty years, and he's played for a number of top managers in his pro career. But if you ask him who his favorite manager is, Curt will quickly point to Mike McQuaid.

(continued))

Curt Schilling's Favorite Baseball Manager

Never heard of Mike McQuaid? Perhaps not. But Curt played for Coach McQuaid when he was in the eighth and ninth grades growing up in Phoenix, and Curt will be the first to tell you what a tremendous positive impact Coach McQuaid had on his game.

"He made it fun to come to practice," recalls Schilling. "He taught us that competing as hard as you can is more important than whether you win or lose. He taught us the lessons I live by today: to always give our best effort and to always be there for our team."

Curt was so impressed with the lessons he learned from Coach McQuaid that in the off-season, when he went back home to Arizona, he asked Coach McQuaid, now fifty-nine, to coach Curt's own nine-year-old son, Gehrig. Notes Schilling: "I wanted Coach McQuaid to have the same impact on Gehrig and his teammates as he had on me."

TRY TO KEEP A BALANCED LINEUP

I do try to be sensitive to the fact that the kids, especially as they get a little older in elementary school, are eager to win their games. For example, when I coach youth basketball, I always make it a point to mix in some of the better players with some of the players who need a little more experience and skill. In short, I try to balance the team. But

I know there are parents in the stands who are wondering, *What in the world is Ripken doing? Why doesn't he just play the five best players?*

To me, it's important that all the kids have a chance to play with all of their teammates, regardless of ability. Plus, if the team is a balanced mix of talent, then in the long run the team will have a better chance to prevail. As the coach, you might want to make this philosophy known to the parents right at the beginning, during your pre-season meeting.

HOW TO HANDLE POSSIBLE FRICTION WITH THE COACH

Even when the kids are still very young, there are, unfortunately, times when there is a difference between what you want for your child and what the coach wants.

Again, this is, for the most part, uncharted territory, since very few of us had our own parents intervene on our behalf when we were growing up and playing on playgrounds and sandlots. But these days, of course, sports parents everywhere are very keen to make sure that their child's coach is treating their youngster in what the parent feels is a proper and positive way.

So what happens if some friction does occur? Or put another way, what's the best way to defuse any coach-parent friction from escalating out of control? We have all heard tales of parents getting in the face of their kid's coach and being totally out of control. To avoid these kinds of ugly situations—whether you're a parent or a coach—there is one constant that must be maintained at all times: *a sense of civility.*

By civility, I mean that you can present your case to the coach, but you have to control yourself and your emotions. You have to pick and choose the time to do this carefully, and you have to most definitely pick and choose your words even more carefully. In addition, there's just no reason to allow your emotions to take over your conversation. Once you let your emotions take over, then the code of civility is lost and the conversation can quickly escalate into a full-blown shouting match or even worse. If you and the coach don't maintain that solid sense of civil behavior between the two of you, then there is very little chance of a positive outcome. And the entire episode will have a negative effect on the child.

Let me give you an example. Suppose your eight-year-old daughter is a soccer player, and, in every game, it's pretty clear to you that the coach is rotating the players around so that they all have a chance to play forward, midfield, fullback, and even goalie. But it seems that the coach has occasionally failed to give your daughter her fair share of playing at the forward position, and she has asked you on numerous occasions at home, "Daddy, how come Coach Smith won't let me play forward more? I want to score more goals . . ."

You have done your best to reassure her that the coach knows what he's doing, and that he has done his best to let all the girls have equal time at the various positions. But then the very next weekend, you watch your daughter play in the game, and sure enough, she plays one quarter of the game at midfield, one quarter at fullback, one quarter as the goalie, and then for one quarter, she sits out. Now she's on the verge of tears for not having a chance to play forward.

As a protective parent who wants the best for his child, you have to decide whether you should say something to the coach as he packs up the soccer balls and other equipment, or wait until tomorrow evening and give the coach a call once you're less emotional about the situation.

Answer? The best approach is to say nothing to the coach about this situation right after the game. You can certainly go over to the coach and congratulate him on a well-played game. **But whatever you do, don't confront him or demand that he speak to you right now about your daughter being cheated out of playing forward.**

The much better—and much more civil—approach is to let yourself cool down and then give the coach a call twenty-four hours later. Even more important, when you do give the coach a call the next night, you must keep the conversation positive and presented in a spirit of cooperation—not one of demands or confrontation. Suppose you were the coach. Would you react better if a parent called you and said:

Listen, Coach, I don't understand why you don't let my daughter play forward . . . You certainly let every other kid play there, even some who clearly aren't very good. So what do you have against my daughter getting her fair share of playing time there?

Or would you like this call better?

Hi, Coach, I'm very sorry to bother you at home, but a matter has popped up in recent weeks with my daughter on the soccer team, and I was hoping to chat with you to see how we could remedy this problem . . .

Of course, there's no question that the second approach is much preferred over the first one. Not only will the code of civility be maintained between coach and parent, but the approach is one of looking for a mutual sense of cooperation. That is, *Coach, we both want the best for the child—won't you help me in finding a solution here?*

And more times than not, when a youth coach is approached in this calm, civil way, not only is the coach very appreciative, but the issue is addressed and the problem is resolved, quickly and painlessly. Again, you're looking for a spirit of cooperation here, not an angry confrontation in which the coach and parent are immediately forced into opposing corners. That accomplishes nothing, except to bruise feelings and cause real ill will between the two.

It's my belief that if more parents and coaches took the time to act like adults, then the vast majority of all these sports-parenting incidents would disappear. If you're looking for a positive outcome for your child, always take the civil approach. In truth, it's the only approach that works!

Let me give you a parallel situation. If you had an issue with your child's teacher in school, about a homework assignment or a grade on a paper, would you rush into the classroom and demand that the teacher speak to you right away about this problem? I'm sure you wouldn't. In fact, I imagine you would first call for an appointment with the teacher, and then when you saw the teacher, you would try and keep the conversation calm and under control. Try that same approach with your child's coach.

SHOULD YOU ALWAYS INTERVENE ON BEHALF OF YOUR CHILD?

Teaching kids that they have to eventually learn how to stand on their own two feet and speak up for themselves is, in my mind, an essential life lesson. But expecting a youngster to know how to approach and communicate his concerns to his coach is probably expecting too much. (That said, by the time your youngster is in high school, you would probably hope that she had enough confidence to know how to speak with her coach on her own.)

But early on, you do have to serve as your child's advocate with the coach. After all, if you don't, who will? That's not to suggest that you should be speaking up for your child with the coach on a daily basis, but when a problem arises that needs to be resolved, there should be no problem with the parent going to the coach directly and having a civil and nonconfrontational conversation.

WATCH YOUR LANGUAGE—PART I

I'm going to focus for a moment on parental behavior, because during youth games, some parents begin to lose perspective on how they act. For example, I would assume you already know that profanity of any kind at these games is simply not acceptable. Swearing is not allowed at any level of youth sports. Period. As an adult who is trying to set a good example, you must conform to this simple rule. *If you can't control your mouth, then don't come to the kids' games.*

Bear in mind that if one of the players utters a swear word during the game, and the umpire or ref or official hears it, then that youngster will either be given a time-out or ejected from the game right away. That rule exists right through youth leagues, high school sports, college, and into the pro ranks. Obscenities are not tolerated, and the sooner you (and your kids) understand and accept that rule, the better off everyone will be.

That said, we all slip on occasion. I did this during one of Ryan's games, and I felt awful. In hindsight, the best thing that I could have done would have been to apologize and leave the area for the rest of the game. That would have sent a message to the kids and the other adults that my behavior was unacceptable and that I wouldn't tolerate it myself.

I probably learned this lesson about parental behavior on the sidelines from my mom. Mom, in her own quiet way, let her behavior set the tone with all of the intense parents and coaches who would come to my games when I was a kid. I remember that the bleachers were right behind the team bench, and the parents were loud and sometimes obnoxious. So Mom started to bring a lawn chair to the games. She placed it down the left field line, well past the bleachers. She was the only one sitting down there by herself for a while, but as the season progressed, I noticed that more and more parents began to join her way down the line. In other words, those parents followed Mom's lead; they also wanted a calmer and less intense environment for their kids who were playing ball. Later, over dinner, Mom would talk about some of the parents and their behavior at the games. And yes, even back then, there would be a few parents screaming and yelling at their kids to play better and not make mistakes. Mom didn't like that, and I certainly understand why. Parents seem to really agonize over their kids competing, but in my opinion, kids need to know how to fail—and their parents need to let them know, and reassure them, that it's okay to fail occasionally. Parents shouldn't agonize over their kids' performance. After all, real learning occurs from mistakes.

WATCH YOUR LANGUAGE—PART II

Not using profanity is a pretty straightforward rule. But I'm also concerned about other forms of verbal interaction that can affect a child during a game.

Let me be more specific. As noted above, it seems that at every game, there will be some parents in the stands who, for some reason, truly expect their kids to play flawlessly. This really bothers me. For example, you will hear a dad up in the bleachers who, after watching his eight-year-old miss a pop-up, bellows out so all can hear (especially his son), "Mike, what are you doing out there!? C'mon, you gotta know how to catch a pop-up! That's an easy out!"

I don't know why a parent would do this to his child. Maybe he is embarrassed that his son missed the ball, and feels compelled to scream at him so that all the other parents at the game will know that he really did teach his son how to catch a pop-up. Or maybe the dad wants so desperately for his son to be a star that he can't control his emotions at the game. But whatever is driving this kind of parental verbal abuse, it is totally unnecessary and totally unacceptable.

Even enthusiastic behavior that is over the top can have a negative impact if you aren't careful. I remember last year when Ryan's team got off to a poor start in a game and they fell way behind. The parents of the opposing team were cheering very loudly and telling their kids how great they were doing. But as the game progressed, Ryan's team mounted a terrific comeback and ended up winning the game. As this was happening, the parents from the other team now became very quiet—so quiet that you could have heard the proverbial pin drop. After all the early innings of boisterous enthusiasm from these parents, their blanket of silence as their kids began to lose sent a poor message to their kids, as if their kids had done something wrong and now their parents were upset with them.

So what should you say if you're a spectator at your kid's game? I suggest saying very little. Just make sure that whatever you say, it's only of a positive nature. Again, kids want to hear praise, and there's no better way to encourage them in a game than by politely rooting for them. Just make sure that you are consistent in your positive behavior because, as illustrated in the story I just related, sudden silence at a kids' game can be deafening!

WATCH YOUR (BODY) LANGUAGE

You may not be aware of it, but your kid will instinctively look up from the field to see you in the stands or on the sidelines to make sure that you are watching her play. When she does something in the game, she is going to look your way right after the play is over. Make sure your body language sends a signal of pride and satisfaction. Kids love parental approval, and nothing builds up their self-confidence more than a big smile from Mom or Dad.

Just as you are watching your child's play on the field, he is watching you carefully in return. If your child makes a mistake or has a miscue—and your body language instantly reflects disappointment or frustration—then your child is going to quickly pick up on that negative image. As you might imagine, that sends him the wrong message. He sees you lower your head, wave your arms in disgust, or kick the dirt, and he instinctively recognizes that he has let you down.

What a terrible message to send to your child! Even if you are saying positive things to your child, your body language of disappointment sends a powerful contradictory message to her. This is sometimes very, very hard to do, but in addition to being cognizant of what you actually say at the games, you also have to be very aware of your body language.

Hey, I'm guilty of bad body language occasionally, too. I recall that this past summer I was perturbed by something that was happening on the field during one of Ryan's games, and I was sitting—I thought—very quietly on the bench. But as soon as Ryan came off the field and saw my body language, he quickly picked up on my being angry. My behavior, just by sitting there, had a direct and immediate impact on him, and he spotted it right away. Once I realized that he was concerned, I immediately assured him that I was not in any way angry with or disappointed in him. So parents, stay in touch with the vibes you're giving off! Kids pick up on the nonverbal cues as much as the verbal ones.

Kids need to have the freedom to learn, to make mistakes, and not be scolded. Kids are always looking for any sign of approval from Mom and Dad on the sidelines. That unconditional approval is key for kids.

Are We Being Good Role Models?

Sports Illustrated for Kids reported in 2001 that almost three-quarters of three thousand of their readers said that they had witnessed out-of-control adults at their games, ranging from parents and coaches yelling at each other, or yelling at kids or officials, to adults who were just downright violent.

Along those lines, the kids who were polled by *SI for Kids* said that the parents' and coaches' constant and heavy emphasis on winning and their being overzealous at youth games were some of the major reasons kids no longer enjoyed playing sports and ended up quitting.

An informal survey conducted by the Minnesota Amateur Sports Commission found that 45 percent of kids said that they had been called names, yelled at, or insulted by adults when playing. Twenty-two percent said that they had been pressured to play even though they were hurt, and an additional 18 percent said that they had been hit, kicked, or slapped while participating.

Other surveys from around the nation as well as from other magazines all report very similar trends in youth sports. No wonder so many kids decide to quit by age thirteen.

DO SILENT SUNDAYS WORK?

Several years ago, in a suburb outside of Cleveland, a number of parents were concerned that parental shouting and yelling from the sidelines during youth soccer games was getting out of hand. To try and bring down the volume, the league instituted an experiment called "Silent Sunday," in which the moms and dads were told to significantly quiet down during the game. Yes, they could applaud for a goal or a nice play, but they were to avoid screaming out instructions to their kids.

No one knew what would happen, but the results were remarkable. For starters, a number of parents recognized that the kids on the field would actually talk and communicate with their teammates during the game. None of the parents had ever heard this before—probably because they were all making so much noise on the sidelines. In addition, on several occasions, the parents could even hear some laughter coming from the kids; again, none of the adults had ever heard the children laugh during a game, because any laughter would have been drowned out by the racket from the sidelines.

Because of the instant success of Silent Sunday, more and more towns have followed the lead. Some leagues even hand out large lollipops or pacifiers to the grown-ups when they come to the games, so that they have something to stick in their mouths instead of yelling and shouting during the game. In fact, it's now become so commonplace that it's the rare town or community that doesn't offer a Silent Sunday. I love the concept and I believe that, when it comes to yelling out instructions during the games, Silent Sundays should apply to coaches as well as parents.

A friend of mine once made a great analogy. He noted that when you are at, say, a piano or dance recital, you don't hear the teacher yelling out instructions from the side, so why do we hear it during an athletic event? Instruction should be given during practice, but when it's time to play the game, that is the kids' time. During the game, I believe that the coaches should observe and take notes, and then use those notes to teach at an appropriate time.

My question is this: *If it's clear that Silent Sunday does, in fact, work in keeping parents in verbal check during their kids' games, why not make every Sunday into a silent one?* Just pass a league rule that parents are not allowed to do anything but clap their hands for a nice play. Yes, Mom and Dad can come to the games and watch and applaud, but wouldn't it be nice just to hear the kids communicate on the field, and not the parents?

Curiously, as popular as Silent Sunday is, I have yet to find a league in which every game is ruled by a Silent Sunday mandate. Apparently, most moms and dads don't mind being quiet for one game, but they very much want the right to cheer loudly at all the other games.

Key Chapter Takeaways

1. If you have any concerns with your child's coach, always remember to approach him or her like you would your child's teacher: with full respect, civility, and with your emotions totally under control.

2. If you're coaching the team, remember this basic rule: Every kid on your team wants one thing—to play a lot in each game. If you can accomplish that, you'll rarely have any complaints from the kids or their parents.

3. Also, if you do serve as the coach, be sure to treat every child in a fair and equal manner. That applies to all the kids on the team, especially your own.

Chapter 4

HELPING YOUR CHILD LEARN TO COPE WITH ADVERSITY

L et me share a story with you about adversity.

As I mentioned earlier, last summer, when Ryan was eleven, he joined a full-bore travel baseball team. He was one of the few new kids on the team, and one of the youngest players. Now, in this team's league, only nine kids can play in the game at a time. That means that two kids have to sit out. And during the first game of the year, Ryan was one of the kids who sat out. Being a competitive kid who was eager to show his stuff, he was upset about this. I really wasn't all that bothered by it; I figured if nothing else it's just a little adversity that will only make him more determined, and build his character a bit. But Ryan really felt embarrassed and deflated by being on the bench.

Kelly was concerned, too. Being a caring and protective parent, she felt Ryan's pain, and she wanted to go and talk with Al, the team's coach, about this situation. But it was only the first game! I tried to point out that this might be a good thing for Ryan.

Al, the coach, had his reasons. It wasn't that he didn't have great respect for Ryan's ability. Al knew that there was a history between these two teams from the summer before. He also knew that Ryan was new to this highly competitive level of ball. So, for the very first game, Al just felt it made sense to ease Ryan in and let him soak up some of the experience from the bench first. It also had the effect of making Ryan that much more determined to do well when he did get his chance.

Sure enough, over the course of the season, Ryan did play. In fact, he played a lot and did well. But that first taste of adversity is something all youngsters (and their parents!) go through.

WELCOME TO THE CONCEPT OF ADVERSITY!

As much as we would prefer that our kids go through their sporting experience without any setbacks, frustrations, or tears, the truth is that every athlete I've ever known—including the top ones—has endured some form of adversity in his or her career. That's just the way it is in sports.

But the good news is that adversity is not necessarily a bad thing. In fact, depending on how your child copes with it, adversity can actually be a wonderful teaching tool and a springboard to getting your child to the next step.

The frustration of striking out several times in a game, or the disappointment of personally allowing a key goal in a soccer game, or just the anger of feeling that one didn't play well in a big game—all of these emotions are absolutely real in youth sports, and most kids show their emotions very easily.

As parents, we all know that our kids will sometimes break into tears if they feel that things didn't go their way that day on the field. Sometimes, children will fight the tears back until they reach the privacy of the family car; sometimes they will cry while still on the field. It makes no difference. As parents, we very much hurt with our children, and we search desperately for something to say that will make their pain go away immediately.

We also know that isn't easy. However, kids will shed their tears for a few moments, hopefully get a solid, supportive hug from you, and perhaps some sincere words of encouragement, and then they move on. But here's the key: Just because the tears go away doesn't mean that the pain of frustration disappears as well. In most kids, the frustration will linger.

Your job is to help them work through this unexpected setback and see if they can channel their frustration into positive and constructive action. But don't rush to do this. That is, give them some space and, as we discussed earlier, let the sting of disappointment stay with them for several hours. Immediately trying to show them how to correct their batting stroke or how to be a better goalie just won't work while their pain is still fresh. If anything, your immediate postgame tutorial will only serve to remind them again of their frustration, and most kids just won't pay any attention. They'll still be too angry!

Instead, wait for several hours, maybe even into the next day. Once you're convinced that your son or daughter is in a better frame of mind, you can then try and have that talk. As always, your approach here is the key. If you are in any way negative or critical in what you say to your child, such as, *Y'know, Joey, if you keep playing that poorly, pretty soon the coach will give you less and less playing time,* then don't be surprised if your child turns away, or even worse, decides that your insights are right on target and gives up! Instead of fighting back against his frustration, he'll just give in and quit. Even if you just try to be objective, as in, *It was pretty clear that you didn't have your best game yesterday,* you will still only reopen wounds in your child.

As such, you have to be very delicate in what you first say to him. The best approach is still one that is laced with praise. Consider this conversation:

DAD: Chris, the truth of the matter is that you actually played a pretty good game yesterday.

SON: Ah, c'mon, Dad, how can you say that? I struck out three times!

DAD: Well, first of all, you made some excellent plays in the field, and on your fourth at-bat, you hit the ball hard for a base hit. That showed a lot of guts, to come back after three tough at-bats to swing the bat and get a hit. Plus, you never gave up. You hustled hard throughout the game, and coaches love to see kids who play hard all the time.

SON: But what about the strikeouts? That was brutal.

DAD: Chris, there are a lot of great ballplayers who are in the Hall of Fame who struck out thousands of times. That's just part of the game, and all the great players know this. The key here is not fretting so much about striking out, but trying to figure out what you can improve upon so that you can hit better in your next game.

By this point, you have gently reassured your son that he's doing just fine, that his overall game was fine, and that striking out is no big deal. But most important, you have opened the door to allow your son to work through his adversity and to work toward improving his batting stroke.

As she gets a little older, you will get a real sense of whether your youngster wants to combat her adversity; whether she has that inner drive and motivation to improve her game. A real key here is whether the child goes out and practices her skills on her own. I find that happening with Ryan. As he gets older, I see him practicing his pick-off moves, or throwing a ball against a wall. I may indirectly introduce him to a few baseball tips here and there, but I don't go over and work with him directly. I let him find his way, according to his own level of motivation.

And then, one day, when he wasn't playing in the game as much as he wanted, he came to me and said, "Dad, could you throw me some batting practice?" That's in direct contrast to so many other parents who, if they see that their kid isn't doing well in the games, immediately go out and hire a private coach for the kid—as opposed to letting the kid come to them. In other words, try not to overreact. Parental patience is a great virtue.

When Sports Aren't Fun . . .

A survey of parents by the National PTA at their major annual convention in 2004 found that 92 percent of the parents polled said that sports were either important or very important to the overall development of their children. That's good! But in that same poll, 44 percent of those same parents revealed that their child had quit playing a sport because it was no longer making him or her happy. Fifty-six percent of the parents said that youth sports had become much too competitive, that the coaches had been much too focused on winning, and that organized youth sports need to be totally revamped in terms of priorities.

TURNING YOUR CHILD'S FRUSTRATION INTO POSITIVE ENERGY

All coaches will tell you that athletes learn more from their setbacks and defeats than they do from triumphs and victories. That's really true. When you win or do well, there is very little impetus to go back out and make adjustments in your game. After all, you won! Why should you change anything?

But when many athletes lose or play poorly, that disappointment burns within them. They don't like to lose. And they don't like to play poorly. So rather than just stew in their juices and sit around feeling sorry for themselves, they will often think about the parts of the game that they want to improve. Before too long, they're practicing on their own, tinkering with their batting stroke, shooting more free throws, or trying to fix whatever part of their game they feel needs help.

There's nothing wrong with reassuring your youngster that frustration is just part of the world of sports. Again, the key is not that she's going to be frustrated occasionally, but rather how she copes with that frustration. You can gently remind your child that the only way to get rid of that inner anger is to go out and practice her game. Only through practice will her skills get better.

If you come home from work one day and find your son practicing on his own in the backyard, then you'll know that you have a child who has that rare inner drive to work through frustration, a kid who is eager to transform disappointment into something positive in his play. Remember, not all kids will do this. The truth is that most won't practice on their own at all. In today's world of structured youth sports, they feel that they only have to work on their sports skills at an organized practice session—a practice called for and run by the coach. If your child is out there practicing his skills on his own in the backyard, this is the right time to praise him again for his effort and determination.

DEALING WITH YOUR KIDS' TEARS

During those times of frustration, kids may deal with adversity by having an emotional outburst. Many parents react strongly in an effort to combat this. They will reprimand their child on the spot because they are embarrassed by his or her behavior.

My parents understood that this was nothing more than misguided passion. My son Ryan is exactly the same way, and I don't think this is a bad thing. I love the fact that he cares so much! The responsibility falls to us as adults to explain to our kids that they need to channel their passion and energy to improve their game. If you can convey that lesson to your child when she is frustrated, her inner drive will become a great and powerful tool for her in the years to come.

PARENTAL EXPECTATIONS AT THIS AGE

While it's perfectly acceptable for moms and dads to feel a great sense of pride when they watch their ten-year-old do well in youth sports, you should try to balance your pride with realistic expectations for your child. That is, celebrate the day—and don't start to worry about what the future might bring.

So if your daughter scores a goal in her soccer game, make it a big deal in your household that night. She'll be happy that she accomplished something very notable on the soccer field, and you want to salute her for that. But once the celebration has ended, move on to tomorrow and leave your expectations behind. There's no reason you should anticipate your child scoring again and again, nor should you start thinking about her becoming the best player in the league.

Can you daydream? Sure. But keep your daydreams to yourself. There's no reason to share them with your child. Besides, once you start talking with your daughter about scoring more and more, then you're unintentionally putting pressure on her to succeed. That's the last thing you want to do. Just let her go out, play her game, have fun, and on those occasions when she does something special, be sure to praise her for it.

But my kid is terrific. . . . She scores every game, and sometimes she scores two or three goals in every game. Everybody can tell she's a cut above the other kids. That's fine. And as her parent, you should be happy about her success. She clearly enjoys playing the game and doing well. And as she progresses through the season, her reputation may spread throughout the community. This is fine and, again, a wonderful development. But it's also no reason for you to start planning for her to earn a college scholarship for soccer.

You have to remember that it's a long, long way through the elementary school, middle school, and high school years. There are just too many variables for you to start planning her athletic career. As kids in elementary school continue to grow and develop, sometimes they develop different interests outside sports. Your daughter may also fall in love with other sports besides soccer. Some kids just get bored and stop playing sports altogether. And the passage through adolescence can change everything, as youngsters go through all sorts of physical and psychological changes during their teenage years.

Remember, in this early developmental time, it all still comes back to passion. You want your child to grow in sports, not just in terms of his ability to master certain athletic skills, but also to get so much enjoyment and fun from his competitions that he begins to look upon his sport as a true passion of his (not yours). You'll see the signs: your daughter's eagerness on game day to get out of bed, get her uniform on, and get over to the game long before it starts; your son's dribbling a soccer ball on his own in the family rec room just for fun; or the self-initiated practice of throwing a tennis ball against a garage door and working on fielding ground balls. When you start to see these telltale signs of passion for a sport, you'll know that your child is developing a real, lifelong love for athletics.

TEACHING GAMES OF SPONTANEOUS FUN

Lots of sports parents today lament the long-gone days of sandlot ball, when we kids used to congregate after school or on the weekends to enjoy pickup games. There were no set teams, no umpires, no league standings, no uniforms, and of course no parents. My brother Billy and I just went out to the closest field, waited to see how many kids showed up, and then had the two oldest kids choose teams. Nobody was excluded from these pickup games, although if you were one of the younger kids, your leadership role was usually limited. For example, if we were playing touch football, and you were a seven-year-old playing with nine- and ten-year-olds, you ended up doing a lot of the hiking of the ball and a lot of blocking to protect the quarterback. As I recall, most of the time it was the older kids who got to play quarterback or were able to run pass routes and catch the ball. (When I was the captain, I usually chose Billy first. That's because even though he was younger, I knew I could get him into the flow of the game and use his skills.)

But the point is, everybody played, regardless of ability. Nobody ever complained, because the younger kids not only learned the game from the older kids, but they also knew that the time would come when they would be the older kids. Sometimes, when there weren't enough kids around to form two teams, we were forced to improvise and devise our own made-up games. We might have impromptu contests of throwing a ball, or rocks, at a target to see who could be the most accurate. Or maybe we would play a game of H-O-R-S-E on the basketball court. Whatever the game we invented, it was just spontaneous fun.

Even today, I look for spontaneously fun games that I can share with my kids and their friends. One of my favorites is a kind of dodgeball that we invented. But instead of using large dodgeballs, we use very soft, spongy baseballs. The kids don't even know it, but as they dash around while playing the game, they're actually working on their foot quickness as well as building their arm strength when throwing the dodge baseballs.

Ironically, now that we're sports parents, we're aware that perhaps our kids haven't developed their own sense of spontaneous fun. Maybe because we introduced them to organized and structured sports leagues at such an early age, they just don't feel any real need to be spontaneous or creative in developing their own games. But if that's true, it's a real shame.

Why not take a moment or two to at least show kids that they can still have fun playing a game even without league standings and uniforms? Maybe you can engage them in a sock-throwing contest. Just ball up some socks, stand back about six feet, and try to toss them, one ball at a time, into a box or container. See if your child will play along with you. Or maybe you can teach him how to play a game of pepper with a bat and ball. Or take your daughter to a soccer field, where you're the goalie and let her try and score on you. Whatever the activity is, by all means make it fun and only a little bit competitive. Remember, it's more about having spontaneous fun than winning.

SIGNS OF EARLY BURNOUT

There are some kids who will become so heavily absorbed in competitive sports at an early age that you might see some indications that their actual passion for athletics is beginning to diminish. As noted earlier, there's a major study out of Michigan State that says that close to three-quarters of all kids who play organized sports will end up quitting them by the time they are thirteen. But even before then, you can be on the lookout for signs that perhaps your child has had enough. Look for the following:

• *Mom, do I have to go to practice this morning? My stomach hurts . . .*

Of course there's always the possibility that your child is coming down with a stomach bug. But how was she feeling last night? Did she sleep well through the night? Does she have a fever this morning? If your parental antennae tell you that there's nothing physically wrong with your child, you might want to suspect that perhaps he's not eager to go to practice this morning and that's why he wants to call in sick. Especially with ailments that are hard to diagnose, such as a stomach hurting, or a headache, or a backache, see if a pattern begins to develop over a couple of practice sessions. More important, see if your child's spirits begin to pick up considerably once you call the coach to tell him or her that your child won't be able to attend the practice.

• *Mom, can I go to Sarah's sleepover party Saturday night? All my friends are going . . .*

There's certainly nothing wrong with sending your daughter over to a friend's home for a sleepover. But you also know from experience that kids rarely get much sleep at these sleepovers, and besides, your daughter has a softball game early the next morning. With little sleep, she'll be in no shape to go out and play in a game.

You can, and certainly should, explain all of this to your daughter. But be prepared when she says she would rather go to the party than worry about the game tomorrow. You have to be aware that her choosing the party over a good night's sleep may be her subtle way of telling you that she might be tiring of too much softball. As a caring parent, you have to be careful how you handle this kind of predicament. If you tell her she can't go to the party and that she has to stay home to sleep, she might retaliate by saying that she doesn't want to play softball anymore.

As a parent who wants the best for your child, see if there is some way that you can work out a compromise solution. Especially with kids under the age of ten, before the concept of real team commitment takes hold, you might be able to find a reasonable end to this dilemma. But one thing is for sure: If your child continues to find ways to avoid games or practices, then you have to come to grips with the reality that perhaps his passion for that sport has diminished considerably.

WHAT ABOUT TEAM COMMITMENT?

There's no question that teaching this concept to kids is one of the essential building blocks of playing youth sports. Being committed to the team and the team's effort should be introduced as soon as kids sign up to play. But that being said, in the ongoing continuum of youth sports from ages five through eighteen, clearly there's a distinction to be drawn between a kid's team commitment at eight and at thirteen.

In general, when kids are ten and under, it's hard to expect that they're going to make every practice and every game on the schedule. When they're that young, and especially if they have siblings, it's going to be very difficult for their parents to get them to every practice and game. Family obligations, such as weddings, reunions, vacations, and the like will invariably conflict with the team's schedule. While you, as a sports parent, will feel uncomfortable telling the coaches about these family conflicts, you definitely owe it to them to let them know well in advance that your son or daughter will not be there for a certain game or practice.

After all, the sooner that the coach knows about these upcoming absences, the more time he or she has to prepare to make alterations to the lineup. Indeed, the worst thing you can do is to wait until the very last second and then tell the coach that your child won't be there. That really is quite inconsiderate to everyone involved, and should be avoided at all costs in fairness to the coach.

Team commitment does begin to get stronger as the youngster gets older, and starts to play sports more seriously. By the time he is twelve or thirteen, your child has to realize (as do you) that making a commitment to the team is going to be more demanding. And by the time she's in high school, there is very little excuse (except for family emergencies) for a youngster missing a team practice or a game. By that point in your child's athletic career, it would be wise to make sure that family vacations and the like are planned so that they don't conflict with the youngster's sports schedule. I recognize that isn't always easy to do, especially when both parents work, there are other kids in the family, and family vacations are planned months in advance, but team commitment grows dramatically as the child gets older and more involved in sports.

It's actually very simple. How would your son feel if he had been working hard all season in the hopes that the team would be in contention come playoff time, only to discover that one or two of the starters on the team decided to go off on vacation? Some parents will argue that family obligations, including vacations, always come first. And while I agree that family certainly does come first, I would also ask whether a little foresight and planning might go a long way toward working around the team's schedule. Remember, for the vast majority of kids, their organized sports career is only going to last until they finish high school, and those seasons go very quickly. Perhaps, for those few brief years, the family vacation can somehow be pushed back to after the season is officially over.

WHAT ABOUT COMMITMENT IN THE EARLY YEARS?

What do you say or do when your six-year-old hops back in the family car after a few games of soccer, and declares: *Mom, I don't like soccer anymore . . . I want to play football instead.*

Your first reaction may be, *Why the sudden change of heart? You've only played three soccer games, you seem to be good at it, and besides, you have all-new soccer equipment and you're with your friends on the same team.*

When kids are just starting out, as six- or seven-year-olds, they really don't know what sport they're going to stick with. You have to give them the opportunity to look around and switch from one sport to another. It's not realistic to expect that a six-year-old will know whether he's going to commit to soccer or football at such an early age, and as a result, the concept of team commitment really doesn't have much impact at these tender ages.

That's not to say that there won't be lots of kids who will definitely commit to their sport, and who will eagerly look forward to every practice and every game. But many younger children may start out playing soccer for a few weeks, then decide they want to try playing tackle football, and then even decide that they want to try running on the local cross-country team. This is all just part of the process of being introduced to youth sports. It's only when they get a little older (around ten) that the idea of staying with one team for an entire season becomes more of a priority.

WHAT ABOUT BOYS AND GIRLS ON THE SAME TEAM?

I can't recall this happening to me when I was playing Little League ball, but I do recall that my brother Billy had not one but two girls on his Little League team. Both of those girls were fine ballplayers and all the boys on Billy's team acknowledged that.

That's why, in my mind, Title IX, which was passed into federal law in 1972, represented one of the great steps forward in athletics in this country. That law made it mandatory that girls have all the same rights in sports that boys have, and it was a most welcome breakthrough.

These days, some thirty years later, Title IX has clearly opened the door to all athletes, regardless of their gender. And even better, for our children, they have grown up in a world where *all* talented athletes are applauded and saluted. That's the way it should be in sports.

As a consequence, at the youth level in many communities, girls and boys routinely participate on the same teams. That's fine. There's no reason to split the kids into two leagues at a young age, because there's very little difference in their athletic abilities at age six or seven. Plus, children these days recognize that all of their schoolmates can be excellent athletes, and as such, they have no problem whatsoever competing against boys or girls. If anybody, it may be some of the more old-fashioned fathers in town who question having all the kids play together.

As with some of the other concepts in youth sports, such as commitment to a team, there is a gradual shift as kids get older in their attitudes about boys and girls playing sports on the same team. In most towns, by the time kids are nine or ten, the local leagues will have teams designated for girls and others designated for boys. This is because as the children grow toward adolescence, gender differences in athletic ability will begin to show, and it will make more sense competitively for the boys to play exclusively on boys' teams and the girls to play on their teams. That's not to say that there won't be some girls who continue to play on the boys' teams. There are plenty of cases of talented girls who prefer to play on boys' teams until they're eleven or twelve—even on travel teams—in order to advance and polish their skills.

Best of all, the boys rarely have an issue with this. If they see that the girl is talented and eager to compete, and can help them win, the boys will be more than glad to have the girl as a teammate. Remember, these days, our kids absolutely get it when it comes to athletic equality between the sexes. It's only us old-fashioned parents who sometimes find ourselves stuck back in the 1960s.

Did You Know. . . .

- That in 2003 there were 3,769 female high school wrestlers in the United States? And that the numbers are growing every year? In most states, female wrestlers still compete on the boys' teams.
- That close to 7,000 girls played ice hockey last year? And most of them played on the boys' team in school?

WHAT ABOUT INDIVIDUAL SPORTS?

Up until now, I have mostly addressed issues that are applicable to kids who play team sports. But there are millions of youngsters who are drawn to individual sports, such as golf, tennis, gymnastics, swimming, wrestling, figure skating, skiing, and many more. Again, it's always hard to predict which sport children are going to be attracted to, but usually by age six or seven, they will be telling you which ones they want to try.

For many parents, there are some inherent concerns about having their child participate in an individual sport. Parents may feel that their child will miss out on the fun and camaraderie of playing with their friends on a team. Or they may worry about the long, isolated hours of practice that go into becoming a top tennis player or swimmer or gymnast. There's even a concern that if the child truly progresses and gives a hint of superior athletic talent by the time she's nine or ten, then the child may be looking at devoting a huge chunk of her developmental years to chasing a dream of perhaps becoming an Olympic champion. It's a long shot, at best, but for lots of kids and their parents, it's a journey worth taking.

To me, the real question is how, as a parent, do you really know whether your child has the potential to become singularly outstanding in his field? I give you some tips and guidelines on how to tackle this issue later in the book. This is a decision that doesn't have to be made right now. In the early years, all that matters is that your child finds a sport or two (or three!) that she enjoys and for which she develops a passion. It makes no difference whether it's an individual sport or a team sport, and of course, it's fine for a youngster to play, say, golf as well as basketball and soccer. The key here is just finding those sports that a child enjoys playing. Have faith in your child.

Parenting Young Athletes the RIPKEN WAY

As he goes through his elementary school years, he will find his way in sports, just as we did when we were his age.

Key Chapter Takeaways

1. How to confront and then work through adversity is an essential lesson that every young athlete has to learn. As a parent, you provide encouragement, but it's up to the child to push herself to the next level.
2. Be careful that you aren't accidentally placing too many expectations on your child when it comes to sports. Otherwise, burnout may result.
3. Commitment to the team becomes a higher priority in a young athlete's life as he gets older.

Chapter 5

TEACHING THE BASICS OF SPORTSMANSHIP

I'm a big believer in the *spirit of the rules* of sport.

That is, when it comes to sportsmanship, there's a certain fundamental, or underlying, spirit of fair and right play that reveals itself in all aspects of competition. Let me give you an example of what I mean.

Every summer, during the Cal Ripken World Series tournament, we always make it a point to speak with all the coaches about the rules. This past summer, Steve Tellefsen, one of the veteran Babe Ruth officials, led the rule discussion and did a fine job. However, one of the youth coaches asked whether there was a penalty for a runner who left first base early (under our league rules, a runner cannot steal a base or leave the base she is on before the ball crosses home plate). Steve said, rightfully, that there was no penalty to be inflicted on the runner.

I could see a number of the coaches raise their eyebrows at this. Realizing that this might lead to some confusion, I decided to stand up and explain the essence of the rule. No, I told the coaches, if a kid leaves early on a pitch, on a steal, there's no penalty. Just put him back on first.

One coach then asked, "Well, what happens if the kid leaves early on a pitch—which is then hit to the shortstop—and the shortstop then throws to second base for a possible force out? But the kid is safe at second, because he left first early."

Under our rules, I explained, the runner is allowed to stay at second.

So then the coach asked, "You mean a kid can leave first early and not be sent back as a penalty?" I began to hear a little more buzz among the coaches. I could anticipate their thoughts—*Hey, maybe I can use this little loophole to my team's advantage in the tournament.*

So I put a halt to this. The truth is, I explained, we can change the rule later, but as coaches, let's not forget the spirit of the rule—and the spirit is that the kids shouldn't leave first early, so please *do not* instruct your kids to do that. Tell them that they should be ready to leave as the pitch goes over the plate, but don't give them the idea to get around the spirit of the rule. That would be the height of bad sportsmanship, and quite honestly, we just don't want kids to compete in that kind of environment.

I looked around the room, and they all agreed. And sure enough, during the entire tournament, there wasn't one incident of that happening. Everybody decided to abide by the spirit of the rule. To me, that speaks volumes about teaching and enforcing good sportsmanship.

That represents the essence of sportsmanship. It's my hope that all parents and youth coaches will always take a moment to ask themselves: What is the spirit of the rule? What is the spirit, or purpose, of the game? In other words, when it comes to kids having fun in sports, what are we truly trying to accomplish?

You, as the coach, need to help them have a good time—make sure that if they lose, it's not the only thing they remember. With Ripken Baseball, in a sense, we're all about transcending the rules. To us, it's all about teaching the game, and honor and respect for one's opponents. Kids have to be taught by both their coaches and their parents to be conscious and aware that every good thing that happens for their team in the game is usually a negative for the other side. Teach kids to be aware of that. That was a lesson that Dad taught us all, and I can assure you I have never forgotten that.

WHAT ABOUT THE INFLUENCE OF TODAY'S PROS?

Kids often copy what they see in the big leagues. That was true when I was a kid, and it's probably even truer today. And I know that kids see lots of awful, unsportsmanlike gestures and actions on the daily televised highlights. Sometimes, the kids copy these gestures in their own youth games. When these events occur, I use those moments of poor sportsmanship as a teaching opportunity. We have to explain to the youngsters what is acceptable and good behavior and what isn't.

This reminds me of a time I behaved poorly when I was a rookie in the big leagues. I struck out and was upset, so I took my helmet off and slammed it to the ground. After the game, Ken Singleton, one of the veteran players on the ball club, took me to the video room and replayed the incident for me. Ken asked me how I thought that looked. I told him that it clearly looked bad.

Ken said, "Look, we all get frustrated at times, but just try to remember that there are kids watching your every move, and acting like that sends them the wrong message." This conversation had a real impact on me, and I always appreciated the fact that Ken cared enough to talk to me about it.

Now, that being said, you do have to give the kids a certain amount of freedom to enjoy their success. All kids do like to celebrate; that's part of the joy of playing competitive sports. Just temper it; make them aware that they don't want their actions to cause any ill will or hurt feelings on the other team.

As a coach or parent, if you do see some of these unsportsmanlike moments occur, take the time to explain to the youngster why it's inappropriate. Just remind her of the Golden Rule as it applies to sports: *Treat the other team in the way that you want to be treated.*

By the way, teaching sportsmanship is an ongoing process, because all sorts of situations can crop up. For example, I don't think you should penalize a kid because he got frustrated after a poor at-bat and threw his helmet down on the ground. In my opinion, discipline should occur not after one incident, but only after a collection of similar incidents. However, the first time the helmet toss happens, make the youngster aware that such behavior isn't acceptable. Much later, after the game, when the emotions have passed, talk to him calmly. Explain things to him. If his actions persist, then let him know that he's not going to be able to play.

In my experience, some kids just don't have the emotional maturity to deal with sportsmanship at a young age. My approach is to try and see if, by talking with the child, you can somehow turn her negative, frustrated energy into positive energy. You really have to teach the child how to manage her feelings.

Let me give you an example. I recall searching for the right opportunity to talk with one youngster—it was two or three days later, after an outburst of frustration on the ball field—and I approached him in a nonthreatening way.

"Not all people have what you have," I told him. "That feeling, that competitive drive inside you." He listened quietly. I said, "If you look at that energy, when you feel that burst, you probably feel like you're the strongest person on the earth. That's positive energy. If you can harness that positive energy, and put it back into your game and control it, that will make you a way better player."

I think I reached him, to a point. The very next day, he gave up a home run, and I could see he was upset, angry, on the verge of doing something unsportsmanslike. But to his credit, this youngster didn't lose his cool. He did a good job at keeping it all under control.

Speaking of discipline and young kids, it's often somewhat difficult to know what kind of punishment should be handed out if a young athlete gets out of hand or breaks a team rule. Whereas a sixteen-year-old would certainly be expected to know what the team rules are, it's not so easy to expect a seven-year-old to know how to behave on a sports field. As a parent and/or youth coach, it's always wise to first take the time to quietly explain to the child why her actions are inappropriate. Then, if she happens to repeat the offensive action, you can ask her to sit out of the game on the sidelines with you.

Let me give you an example. Whenever Sally, a talented young soccer player, scores a goal, she has a habit of running up to the goal net, retrieving the ball, and kicking it into the goal again. She does this only to celebrate her goal, as though she's putting an exclamation point on it.

As you might imagine, the opposing teams and goalkeepers don't much care for Sally's celebratory antics, especially if she happens to score a couple of goals in the same game. As Sally's coach, you feel a responsibility to say something to her about good sportsmanship.

YOU: Sally, there's no question that you are a very talented soccer player. It must be a lot of fun to score those goals.

SALLY: Yes, Coach, it sure is . . .

YOU: Sally, I know you're just starting out on your soccer career, but as your coach, I have to caution you that when you retrieve the ball from the net and then kick it in again, that's really not good sportsmanship.

SALLY: But, Coach Smith, all of my friends think that's very cool . . . it's like my signature move.

YOU: I understand, Sally, but you have to put yourself in the role of the other team's goalie. She's trying her best to play well, too, and when you score a goal, that goalie already starts to feel bad about letting down her teammates. And then, when you emphasize the goal by kicking the ball in again, it just leaves a bad taste in everyone's mouth. It's just not an acceptable display of positive sportsmanship.

SALLY: Okay, Coach, I'll try and cut back on it a little bit.

YOU: Uh, Sally, I don't think you understand. While I certainly want you to go out and have fun and score goals, I really can't allow you to keep doing this second-goal celebration. If you do it again, I'll have to ask you to sit here on the sidelines with me until you fully understand the lesson of sportsmanship that we're trying to teach.

This conversation shouldn't last more than a couple of minutes, and it should be delivered in a calm, patient manner. Remember, you're educating a youngster about the rules of sportsmanship, and the truth is, she may not have been aware of what is acceptable behavior and what isn't. That being said, once she has been spoken to, if Sally does repeat her actions, then the only effective way to get her attention for good is by having her sit out. And not just for a couple of minutes, but for a good long stretch of the game. Have her stand next to you, and let her observe you as you keep putting other players into the game. After a while, if Sally is like the vast majority of other competitive athletes, she'll start asking you when she can return to the game.

When she does ask that, you can then turn to her and simply ask, *Sally, have you learned your lesson about good sportsmanship? If yes, then I can return you to the game. But if I ever see you doing something unsportsmanlike again, then I will take you out of the game and have you watch indefinitely. Do you understand?*

With young kids, because they are so eager to get back into the action, ideally the lesson will be learned, and learned for the rest of their playing days.

WHAT IF HER PARENTS OBJECT TO HER BEING DISCIPLINED?

Don't be surprised if Sally's mom or dad ambles over to you and asks why she is sitting out of the game. Even worse, sometimes the parent will actually approach you during a break in the action or at halftime. If this occurs, as the coach, you have to calmly and patiently explain to the parent that his or her child did something that was inappropriate, and as a result, she is being given a time-out to correct the situation. Then tell the parent that you will be glad to discuss the situation in more detail at a later time, but that *right now during the game* is not an appropriate time.

Above all, do not become confrontational with the parent. Just give a reassuring look and tell the parent again that you'll be glad to discuss his or her child's actions a little later on, after the game.

When the time is right, of course most parents will want a more detailed explanation of what happened, and you should provide it to them. But try and downplay the incident. Rather than alarm them or upset them, just let them know that learning about sportsmanship is a natural part of the growing process in sports, and that their child is merely learning from this incident. Assure the parent that his or her child has learned her lesson and will resume her normal playing time in the games to come.

WHAT IF YOU'RE THE PARENT WHOSE KID IS DISCIPLINED?

As mentioned earlier, sportsmanship is a life lesson that should be introduced to your child long before he actually plays in an organized youth league game. If you have done your homework as a parent, your child should already have a good idea of what's acceptable and what isn't when it comes to his behavior in games. More important, it's critical that while you have parental sympathy for your child's misbehavior, you also make it clear that you fully support the coach's position. If you don't, or if you tell your child in the car ride home that the coach is wrong, then you're going to plant the concept in his mind that he doesn't always have to listen to his coach, that indeed he can question the coach's authority, and most important, that it's okay to flaunt the rules of sportsmanship.

So be careful. The early years are the developmental years, and you definitely want to make sure your child takes away the right lessons for life regarding not only sportsmanship, but also how to respect the coach, the ref, and one's opponents. Many times you will see unsportsmanlike behavior at the professional level of sports, and you just wonder whether these top athletes were ever instructed on how to behave well when they were younger. Again, sportsmanship is a lesson that should be taught, learned, and enforced in your child's sports career so that the lesson stays with him for a lifetime.

OUR OWN ROOTS REGARDING SPORTSMANSHIP

In order to get a better grasp of how the concept of sportsmanship is so embedded in us, allow me take you down memory lane for a few moments. When Billy and I were growing up in Maryland, every day was a new day for us in terms of playing sports. Depending on the season, we played all sorts of pickup games with our friends and buddies from the neighborhood. There's a good chance you had a similar background as a kid.

To be sure, it was a different time and place, where kids stayed out on the playground all day in the summertime, until Mom called us home for dinner. Unfortunately, I don't think those innocent days of our youth are ever going to come back. Kids' sports today, as we all know, have just become too organized, too structured, and of course too overrun by well-meaning moms and dads.

But there are some lingering legacies from our childhoods that stick with us. And some of these legacies are vitally important when it comes to how we understand sports and, in particular, how we learned about the concept of sportsmanship. When we were kids and showed up on the playground, usually the two oldest kids would become de facto team captains. Then, the two captains would choose two equal teams so that the game would be competitive and evenly matched.

There was no need for a parent to be there to supervise this choice of players. All of us kids knew right away which kids were the fastest, or the biggest, or who had the best arm, or who was the best at catching a ball, and so on. So it was usually a fairly quick and painless process for two equal teams to be selected. I can't recall anyone ever complaining.

But here's the interesting part of this process. Let's say it was a touch football game and both teams had four kids. Suppose one team quickly jumped out to a three-touchdown lead, and it was clear to everyone that the game was going to be a lopsided one. What did we do? Invariably, the game came to a unanimous halt, and the two captains got together and started to mix and match players from the two teams. Why? So that the game could then continue, but with squads of more equal ability. As I recall, no one protested, because all of us kids knew instinctively that it was always a lot more fun to play in a game that was competitive and that featured a close score than to play in a game in which the score was one-sided.

In addition, along those same lines, we also knew that it wasn't much fun to have another team run up the score on our team. Nobody wanted to play on a team that was being humiliated, and likewise, it wasn't much fun to play on a team that could score at will on its opponent. We learned early on that in order to enjoy winning, you needed to have a worthy opponent. If you could win easily, well, then there was no fun in the challenge.

All of us kids recognized that keeping the score close was the absolute key to how much fun everyone would have. It was in everybody's best interest to have both teams be equal in ability. That's why games would stop and have teams reassessed whenever the score got out of hand.

Those simple lessons from our childhoods actually serve as the basis of how we perceive sportsmanship today. Specifically, everybody wants to play on a team that has as good a shot at winning as every other team in the league. And secondly, a game in which the score gets out of hand is no fun for anyone, the winners or the losers. Not surprisingly, our kids also instinctively want the same basic principles of good sportsmanship.

Curiously, though, sometimes parents and coaches seem to forget the basic lessons of sportsmanship. Too many youth coaches lose perspective and don't seem to realize that running up the score is not acceptable or fun for any of the kids on the two teams. Or at the league's team meeting when the coaches first get together to go over the drafting of teams in the league, there's too much of a competitive drive to make sure that one's team is superior to all of the others. Sports parents today seem determined to make sure that in terms of overall talent their kid's team has the edge over every other team in the league. Why? So that their kid's team can be league champions, of course!

WHY THE CONCEPT OF "DO-OVERS" IS STILL IMPORTANT

There are other valuable lessons regarding sportsmanship that we seem to have lost along the way. When I was a kid, if my brother and I were playing in, say, a pickup basketball game, and there was a close play—let's say I was driving to the basket with the ball, and as I did, I tried to put up a layup, and Billy fouled me on my arm—then the action would stop momentarily while I called the foul and asked for the ball back to resume play. But if Billy protested and insisted that he didn't hit my arm at all, but only made contact with the ball, then very quickly a minor squabble would pop up.

"Billy, you definitely hit me on my arm . . . It's a foul!"

"No, Cal, I only hit the ball . . . I never touched your arm!"

After a minute or two of back-and-forth, the other basketball players would realize that neither Billy nor I was going to budge, so someone would suggest a *do-over.*

Now, if you're reading this book, you're probably old enough to remember what a do-over is. Basically, it's a simple and quick understanding that the previous play is in dispute, and that it can't be resolved by either team. As such, to keep the game going, we might as well start again, as though that disputed play never happened. In effect, we're going to just erase that play and move on.

Do-overs were an everyday part of playground life for all of us growing up. But what perhaps we didn't understand at those young ages is that our mutual ability to reach a compromise and to resolve a conflict peacefully is also one of the absolute fundamentals of sportsmanship. This life lesson became programmed into our way of not only playing sports, but also of approaching other conflicts in life—i.e., to always try to find a compromise. Indeed, in many respects, sportsmanship itself is all about compromise. That is, if your child is going to play competitive sports, then you and your child have to learn how to cope with both winning and losing. After all, sometimes you win, and sometimes you lose.

Even more significant, when you engage an opponent in a debate about a disputed call in a youth game, and it becomes clear that he is not going to back down from his position, you have to learn to accept that your opponent's viewpoint is just as worthy as your own. You may not agree with it; indeed, you may insist that the opponent (or the ref or ump) is all wrong. But either way, you have to accept that he has a different point of view. Again, that's part of learning good sportsmanship. Trying to see the game from the opponent's perspective builds youngsters' sense of respect for the other team.

One of the by-products of playing on pickup teams that are chosen on a daily basis is that you get to know not just a few select friends from your neighborhood but all the kids. For example, in Monday's touch football game, you might be teammates with Sal, Eric, and John. But in Tuesday's game, your teammates are Mike, Matt, and Monte; in fact, those guys just happened to be your opponents during Monday's game!

Here again, the young athlete gets to know *all* the kids as possible teammates, and once again, that goes a long way in enforcing good sportsmanship. Why? Because most kids like to treat their friends and buddies in a positive way, much in the same way that they want to be treated.

Back to do-overs. One of the sad realities of youth sports today is that kids don't have to learn about do-overs. Unlike when we played on the sandlots, in today's youth sports leagues, there's always an umpire or referee or official to make every call in their games. Kids may not like a call, and may even want to argue about a ruling, but there's no room or time for a debate or a do-over. Once the call is made, the game goes on. Our children are instructed to play on. And as the game proceeds, I fear that our kids' opportunity to learn from the compromise of do-overs fades away.

Am I suggesting that we should do away with umpires and refs? Of course not. But I do want to point out that, bit by bit, we have accidentally eliminated a great many opportunities for our kids to learn about sportsmanship and respect for their opponents.

PLAYING BY THE RULES—DO CHEATERS PROSPER?

One of the other long-lost principles of our youth is that everyone naturally expected everyone else to play by the rules. Cheating was not acceptable under any circumstances. Let me make this very clear: *There's no honor, or any sense of accomplishment, when you cheat in sports.*

If we, as kids, did suspect an opponent of cheating during a pickup game and he didn't come clean, then the ultimate (and final) solution was for us to walk away and end the game. But since no one wanted the game to end, and since you couldn't have a game if one of the teams didn't play, cheating rarely occurred.

Besides, all of us kids were absolutely convinced of the age-old proverb, "Cheaters never prosper." As I recall, no one ever really provided any proof that backed up this maxim, but all of us accepted it as the gospel truth. And because everybody believed that cheating was the worst thing you could do in sports, it's hard to recall when any of our friends did cheat.

These days, though, with today's grown-ups, I'm afraid that proverb has become somewhat modified. Now it seems that "It ain't cheating unless you get caught" is the law of the land. Whether it's a youth baseball player whose parents lie about her birth date, or parents who try to jerry-rig the draft selection process so that their kid lands on the "best" team, or parents who find a loophole in the league bylaws that will benefit their kid, we have now become a nation where too many sports parents seem to be always searching for that edge, that extra advantage, to help propel their child to the winner's circle.

When I hear about these kinds of situations, I know that ultimately it's the kids who pay the price. All I want to do is remind today's parents that "Cheaters never prosper." That was sound advice when I was a kid, and it still makes a lot of sense today.

WHAT PARENTS REVEAL ABOUT THEMSELVES
AND SPORTSMANSHIP

In a previous chapter, I discussed your language and actions at your kids' games and how kids pick up quickly and instinctively on your actions. Well, the same principle applies to how your kids learn about sportsmanship from you.

Let's say you're at your daughter's softball game and she strikes out on a called third strike that she felt was way out of the strike zone. First she's surprised and then angry about the call. She immediately looks over to the sidelines, only to see you look down with disappointment, kick the dirt in disgust, and then yell something mean, angry, and not very sporting to the umpire. Ask yourself: How do you think she's going to react to an umpire the next time a call doesn't go her way?

If a call by the ref goes against your child's team, and your kid looks over to the sidelines and sees you throw an absolute tantrum or scream and yell something like *C'mon, ref, that's not fair! You gotta call 'em equal for both sides!* or words to that effect, your child will immediately get a conflicted message.

On one hand, your child has been instructed during practices and before games to have only the highest respect for the refs and of course to be a good sport at all times, even when there's some adversity on the field. But now, during the course of an actual game, that same youngster is seeing that his mom or dad is going bonkers when a call goes against him.

So what kind of response would you expect your child to have to all of this? Will she continue to strive to be a good sport? Or will she learn that all that talk about good sportsmanship is nothing but a bag of hot air—and that she should follow her dad's example and protest every bad call during a game? Clearly this is a decision that will influence your child and her teammates in the years to come, so please think about how you look and behave at your kids' games.

Even worse, the truth is that most parents don't ever realize how they appear to their kids. Let me give you an example. Sometimes someone will bring a video camera to a youth game, so that his or her child's action on the field can be viewed later. That, of course, is fine. But what I always find extraordinarily revealing is when that videotape is played back later and you happen to see parents on the tape. They're shouting, jumping, running around, and occasionally throwing their arms and hands up in disgust when a call goes against their child or their child's team. Remember that lesson I learned from Ken Singleton when he showed me a video of me losing my temper in my rookie year?

When parents watch themselves on tape, they at first begin to laugh out of embarrassment, but after a while, the laughter fades away. It finally begins to sink in what kind of message their frantic actions are sending to their kids. It can be a most enlightening moment for these parents.

These kinds of videotapes can be so revealing that I'm tempted to suggest that youth leagues make it a standard practice to occasionally tape the parents during their kids' games. Then make sure that all the moms and dads watch the tape later on. Trust me, they'll be shocked and embarrassed by their behavior patterns. And even worse, the kids all pick up on these unsportsmanlike cues.

SPORTSMANSHIP AND ZERO-TOLERANCE POLICIES

In recent years, because the volume of verbal outbursts and taunts from parents in the stands has reached all-time highs, more and more youth leagues have actually resorted to adopting zero-tolerance policies for parents and coaches. This is a sad development, to be sure, because it means that the grown-ups at the kids' games have lost sight of how to behave, or of what's acceptable and what isn't.

Zero tolerance basically gives the umpire, ref, or official the absolute power to stop the youth game at any time and point to the offensive individual on the bench, on the sidelines, or in the stands, and simply announce: *Folks, unless the man over there in the third row and green shirt gets up and leaves the ballpark within the next five seconds, then this game will immediately cease, and I will award a forfeit to the other team. Sir, you have five seconds to leave the premises . . . starting now.*

This is zero tolerance in action. In those leagues where zero tolerance is in effect, the ref or ump has every right to do this. After all, there's no reason for a parent to berate and harass a ref, most of whom are working the game either as volunteers or for just a few bucks. Even worse, most of these out-of-control loudmouths ruin the experience for everyone else as well, including the kids.

So when those five seconds begin to tick away, here's what inevitably happens. All the other spectators and kids on the field will turn around and immediately watch to see what the accused parent will do. The parent is thus placed under tremendous peer pressure. That is, if he decides to ignore the ref's dictate to leave, then the parent knows that the ref will indeed call the game off.

Ask yourself: How would you like it if your son's game was forced to end prematurely and be a forfeit because some dopey parent couldn't keep his or her mouth shut? Chances are you and the kids would be pretty angry.

That's precisely why the accused parent will ultimately decide to get up and go, so that the game can continue without interruption. And sometimes, when he does finally leave, there will even be a spontaneous round of applause from all the other spectators, who are glad to see that he's gone for good. The tricky part, of course, is making sure that the officials are fair in their treatment. They have to maintain their perspective and not toss out any parent or fan indiscriminately.

Those communities that have adopted zero-tolerance policies have to do a lot of preseason work to get the word out to the parents. Usually a one-sheet handout is mailed to all the parents in the league, or is posted on the league Web site, so that everybody knows about it. Sometimes, right before the game begins and the teams take the field, the ref or ump will also turn to the assembled parents in the stands and remind them that this game is a zero-tolerance game, and the policy will be strictly enforced.

Yes, being kicked out of your child's game is a harsh penalty, but for those towns that now use a zero-tolerance policy, it has clearly cut back on the unsportsmanlike behavior of the parents at their kids' games. It's too bad that we have come to this, but the alternative is having too many grown-ups at youth games who are out of control. Besides, it's just not fair to the refs and umps and officials. Why should they have to bear the brunt of obnoxious comments from parents and coaches?

WHAT YOU SHOULD KNOW ABOUT TRASH TALKING

Trash talking is another one of those modern-day phenomena that didn't exist when we were kids. Clearly it's not something that is to be encouraged with young athletes, even though they may see some of their sports heroes doing it during televised games. Trash talking runs totally counter to the concept of good sportsmanship, so if you happen to see your youngster or her friends beginning to engage in this kind of activity, put an end to it right away.

Another example of poor sportsmanship is when one ball club will initiate various loud chants or even songs on the bench, all designed simply to distract the opposing pitcher or players in some way. Some coaches actually encourage this kind of verbal behavior—*Hey, let's hear some enthusiasm from you kids on the bench!*—but while it's fine to have the kids cheer for their teammates, you're really stepping over the line of sportsmanship when the cheering turns into chants and bench-jockeying songs.

Remind your youngster that verbal put-downs, taunts, and teasing are never acceptable and that they reflect very poorly on him and his teammates. And tell him not to be surprised if his coach benches him if he continues with such negative behavior. In short, there's no reason for trash talking at any time.

Key Chapter Takeaways

1. **Proactively teach your kids about the lessons of sportsmanship, and how to behave appropriately, after they win or lose a game. Explain to them that what they see during televised sporting events may not always be the right example of good sportsmanship.**

2. When it comes to sportsmanship, always remind kids of the Golden Rule: Treat your opponents the way you'd like to be treated.

3. Remind kids that playing in the game is a privilege, not a right. And if they don't behave properly, then they will lose that privilege.

Chapter 6

PROS AND CONS OF TRAVEL TEAMS

Travel teams didn't exist when I was a kid growing up. The concept just hadn't been invented yet, or if they did exist, nobody in my town knew about them. But of course, these days, travel teams have spread across the country everywhere, and indeed, it's the rare community that doesn't offer travel teams for kids in a variety of sports.

Travel teams are also known as select, elite, premier, or even club teams. Sometimes they are just comprised of kids from one town who made the league all-star team. Other travel teams are composed of kids who went through rigorous tryouts before the season in order to make the team. Regardless of what they are called in your town, the concept is the same. These teams are meant to be a step up in terms of attracting those kids who seem to have a little more athletic ability and a little more desire to work at their sport, and who have parents who can

Caution: Time Management and Travel Teams

According to a study just completed by Columbia University, teenagers who eat dinner with the rest of their family at least five times a week are more likely to get better grades in school and much less likely to have substance abuse problems. According to the study, only about half of American teenagers say that they have regular family dinners.

In effect, the study suggests that family time may be more important to children than many parents realize. Specifically, teens who sit down to family dinners five or more times a week were 42 percent less likely to drink alcohol, 59 percent less likely to smoke cigarettes, and 66 percent less likely to try marijuana. Frequent sit-down dinners were also correlated with better performance academically in school, with teens 40 percent more likely to get As and Bs if they dined with their family. In a related study conducted at Harvard University, family dinners were the most important events in helping children develop their language skills.

devote the time, energy, and money to let their kid be on the team.

Travel teams usually have much different agendas than the local recreational programs that most towns have—in which all kids are given equal playing time regardless of ability, and in which the atmosphere is much less competitive. For starters, the time commitment is more substantial. A rec team might have one game every weekend for eight Sundays, and there might be one practice each week. Once the rec season ends with the last game, that's pretty much it until the next rec sport season begins.

In contrast, a travel team will usually have at least two practices during the week, plus at least one game per weekend, and often two or more. There are usually tournaments to play in over long weekends, to which the team has to travel a long distance, as much as an hour to several hours by car. Travel team seasons are much longer than the rec leagues'. With some sports, being on a travel team means making a serious commitment for the entire fall, into the winter, and then all spring as well.

Travel teams don't usually have the same restraints about equal playing time for all team members. The emphasis often shifts right away to winning. That shift can definitely benefit your child if she is one of the better players on the team, since she'll start to enjoy more playing time. But such a system can also backfire if your child isn't considered one of the top players on the team. He may end up sitting on the bench a lot more than he wants.

A commitment to a travel team will mean having to plan your family's schedule weeks in advance, especially if you have more than one child who plays sports. Bear in mind that kids on travel teams can't drive themselves to their practices and games, especially if they are road games. That means you have to be available to do the chauffeuring several days a week, and especially on the weekends.

Finally, travel teams cost money. Unlike the local rec team, which might cost $50 to $100 for registration and uniform, a travel team, depending on the sport, can cost anywhere from $500 to as much as $2000 or $3000 for the year. Traditionally, ice hockey travel teams are the most expensive, because in addition to the expensive equipment and the coach's stipend, parents also have to chip in to pay for the ice rental. But that's not to say that the other travel sports are going to be inexpensive. It's always a good idea to find out up front what the cost is projected to be for your son or daughter's participation in a travel team.

THE GOOD NEWS ABOUT TRAVEL TEAMS

There are many positive aspects of travel teams. They offer development and opportunities for kids to have fun playing with other kids who have similar athletic abilities. For example, if you're playing shortstop and the kid playing second base doesn't have the ability yet to catch a ball that you've thrown to him, you're going to find that very frustrating. For a kid, it's really great when she can turn a double play for the first time because the second baseman can catch the ball, make a pivot, and throw a solid strike over to first. A travel team can offer this kind of excitement to young players a lot more often than a local rec team can. I can recall when I was a kid, playing on an all-star team was something like being on a travel team. I always enjoyed it because I knew I was playing on a team with other kids my age who could run, throw, and hit.

All that travel time in the car is a wonderful chance for you to bond and communicate with your child. Although I didn't play on a travel team as a kid, I do recall spending time with my dad when he would have to go on the road to do clinics in the off-season. Dad was an excellent listener, and I would talk to him on those car rides. I did most of the talking—he would ask the questions. And he never lectured me. To this day, I still treasure those moments of just him and me talking, father and son. Car time can be the greatest time you can spend with your kid.

But travel teams cause some concerns as well. My dad always used to say, "All good things in moderation," and certainly travel teams fall into that category. There has to be a commonsense judgment by you as to what is in the best interests of your child's health and development. Travel teams are not bad, but they can be overdone and become negative.

For example, on a travel team, should only the best players play? Well, the game *is* a competition, and there's a constant conflict between wanting to win and the development of each player's skill. I am very concerned that the emphasis on a travel team can easily slide from the development of kids into an overriding desire to win. I've seen that happen too often with travel teams and it definitely concerns me.

Let me explain what I mean. In professional baseball, the vast majority of major league organizations have this overriding philosophy: Minor league baseball is about player development first and winning second. That is, developing young talent is more important in the minors than winning a minor league championship.

For example, a minor league manager might have a situation late in a tie game in which he knows that a young player is coming to bat. The manager knows that it's his job to develop that young player's talent; that is, to get him accustomed to batting in a clutch situation. Yes, the manager could pinch-hit for the young player with an older, more experienced batter, but if he did that, the manager wouldn't be doing his job in terms of *player development*. In my opinion, that same philosophy should apply to travel teams as well. Sure, every team and coach wants to win, but the real top priority should be player development.

IS WINNING THE TOP PRIORITY?

While I understand that, for kids over the age of twelve, winning does take on a greater importance, I do worry about this shift in priority.

For example, this past summer when Ryan was playing for his baseball travel team, as the season came down to the final tournament, the rules made it clear that the coach could bring in an extra player or two if he wanted.

Ryan's coach, who is a terrific and caring fellow, clearly agonized about whether he should bring in a ringer to play for his team, the Baltimore Buzz, and he asked the team parents for their thoughts. At that time, the coach did his best to explain that the new player would most likely be used in a utility player kind of situation; that is, as a player who would fill in on occasion. But as it developed, the new kid's presence on the team did cost some of the regular players at-bats that they would have gotten if he hadn't been added to the roster.

As you might imagine, this is just the kind of issue that can divide the team and the parents. The travel team coach has the right to say, *Other teams are bringing in top all-stars to the tournament. We have the same right to do that, and I think we should if we want to have a serious chance to win.* But the parents, especially if their kid already isn't getting much playing time, are now facing the prospect of seeing their kid get even less, despite the expense of time and travel to the tournament. I think the coach has to be very, very careful about making this kind of late-season move. And if the coach does bring the extra kid in, he has to be very open and honest with the parents about what the impact of that new player will be on the playing time of the current kids. If the coach isn't clear about what is going to happen, then this is a sure bet for developing team dissension.

I'm not sure that there's a perfect solution to this kind of situation, but clearly it's one of the issues that often accompanies life on a travel team.

WHO'S RUNNING THE TRAVEL TEAM?

Unlike the local youth leagues, whose coaching staffs are stocked by parents who simply volunteer their time to help out, travel teams are usually set up and run by either an independent coach who has a background in that sport or by a parent in the community who wants to help the better athletes get on a more accelerated course in youth sports. As you might suspect, more often than not, that parent usually has a son or daughter whom he or she feels is talented, and who is also eager to play at a more competitive level.

You should also note that pretty much anyone can announce to the community that he or she is going to set up a travel team. Unlike local rec teams, which are usually organized and overseen by either a national group (such as American Youth Soccer Organization, Pop Warner Football, USA Hockey, and so on), or overseen by the local parks and rec program in your town, individual travel teams aren't bound or legislated by those operations. If your son or daughter gets a flyer in the mail, or hears in school about a new travel team offering tryouts, it would certainly behoove you as a prudent parent to do a little advance homework about the team, the coaching staff, their priorities, their schedule, and their fees.

First and foremost, you want to find out who's running the travel team. Not only do you want to know the person who's organizing it, you also want to know his or her background in that sport (especially the coaching background), who is actually going to be coaching the team on the sidelines, and who the assistant coaches are going to be. Remember, most travel teams are going to be started by a local parent who wants his or her son or daughter to benefit from playing against better competition. As you might imagine, it's the rare travel team coach who doesn't automatically give his or her own child the starting nod at the kid's favorite position. That's something to keep in the back of your mind if the coach's kid is a first baseman, and that's the position your son plays as well.

Al McGuire, the legendary basketball coach at Marquette University, was once asked about a situation in which his son and another basketball player were competing for the last spot on the Marquette team. McGuire, in his traditional outspoken way, simply said—and admittedly I'm paraphrasing him here—"If the last spot on the team is between my son and another kid, then that other kid better be a whole lot better than my boy, because if they're equal in ability, the tie goes to my flesh and blood."

I respect the candor of Coach McGuire, and for better or worse, that same philosophy is in place on most travel teams. Clearly the driving force for the parent to organize the team in the first place is to put his or her son or daughter on the athletic fast track. That's fine, so long as the parent is fair about the evaluation of his or her kid and the other kids on the team. More than that, you really want to know the coach's background. Did they play the sport at an advanced level; that is, beyond high school and into college or even in the pros? Once their playing careers were over, did they coach successfully in other programs? Just how closely are they involved with the sport? Do they really know how to work with younger players?

What is the coach's general reputation in town? As a yeller and screamer? Or as a kind and patient person? Is the coach's reputation one of being fair and honest, or as one of those people who want to gain every advantage possible, just so that their team can win? These are the kinds of basic questions that every parent should be asking if his or her child is thinking of trying out.

ARE THE TRYOUTS FAIR AND HONEST?

Speaking of tryouts, you owe it to your youngster and yourself to find out about how the kids are evaluated in the tryouts. If the tryouts are run by the travel club owner/coach and his assistant coaches (who, by the way, most likely have their own kids who want to be on the travel team), just assume that those kids will immediately make the squad, regardless of their ability. So if the travel team has twelve kids on it, perhaps four slots will be automatically taken by the kids of the coaches. That may not be fair, but more times than not, that's how it works.

Along those same lines, you might discover that there are two or three other talented athletes in town who were specifically approached before the tryouts and asked by the travel team coach to play on the team. That means that two more slots are now taken, leaving only six. Presumably, your child—along with as many as twenty or thirty other kids—will be trying out for six open slots. And you won't know how many "friends of friends" of the coach's kid will be given every opportunity to make the team as well.

If all of this sounds a bit cynical, please know that I'm not trying to be negative here. I'm only trying to be honest with you so that you and your child can make an educated decision as to whether going out for a travel team makes sense for him. Especially with kids under the age of twelve, what your child *really* needs more than anything else is a combination of playing time and self-confidence. If he can get that from the travel team, that's great. But if he can be assured of that from playing on the local rec team, then let him play there, let him enjoy himself, and let him build his confidence. Remember, athletes don't improve their game skills by sitting on the bench!

If you have ever had a child go through a tryout for a travel team, you know firsthand how emotionally grueling this can be. I know of one town in Connecticut where ice hockey is extremely popular with the kids, but because of limited ice time, the local travel team has openings for only seventeen kids each year. Unfortunately, as many as eighty kids show up for the tryout. Because there's real concern about nepotism and other kinds of favoritism being shown, the travel team board of directors came up with an intriguing way of keeping the tryouts fair and square.

The board went out of state, in this case to Rhode Island, and hired a group of six hockey evaluators to come to their town for two weekends and do the evaluations. To keep it honest, all young hockey players were given a sheet of paper with a printed number to wear on their back. Kids were instructed not to wear jerseys that had their names on the back, or any kind of logo on the front that suggested where they had played the last season. If they did, they were not allowed on the ice.

From there, the kids went through their paces on the ice for several sessions. The Rhode Island coaches were huddled by themselves, far away from the nervous parents, so that anxious moms and dads couldn't approach them and spy on how their kid was doing. When the tryouts were completed, the Rhode Island evaluators give a list of the seventeen best players they saw to the board of directors, and then the numbers were matched with the kids' names. That became the travel team.

Now, that might seem like an extreme example of how to ensure the tryouts for a travel team were done fairly. But in this particular town, where emotions run strong about the youth hockey players, this process worked. No one could complain of any favoritism or nepotism influencing which kids made the team.

Does that mean that the travel team tryouts in your town should be run the same way? Maybe or maybe not.

But I think all parents would want to make sure that their child gets a fair and objective chance. If there are only so many slots available, you don't want to discover that several of them were already filled by friends of the coach's kid. Again, go back to sportsmanship: In the spirit of the rules of the game, everybody wants, and should get, a fair and equal chance.

WHAT'S THE RIGHT AGE FOR MY KID TO TRY OUT FOR A TRAVEL TEAM?

Remember this: *Whether your child plays on a travel team at age seven or eight makes no difference in her ultimate development as an athlete.* I know there's a tremendous amount of parental pride in saying that your child made the travel team when he was eight, but if being on that team means that he's going to get limited playing time, or if he doesn't feel he's ready to compete against the other kids on the travel team, the entire experience might actually sour him on staying with that sport! Wouldn't he have more fun and be better served if he played on the rec team? Ryan didn't play on a travel baseball team, the Baltimore Buzz, until he was eleven years old.

The reason I mention this is that too many times a travel team coach will openly explain to all the travel team parents at the first practice that his philosophy is that the better and/or more experienced kids on the team are going to get the most playing time. Yes, everybody will get some time in the games, but it probably won't be equal. Of course, for most parents, since they already consider their child to be one of the top players on the team, this coaching philosophy is fine—because they truly expect their own child to get a lot of playing time.

The problems usually erupt around the third or fourth game, when it becomes clear that their child is on the bench more often than not, or that she's getting playing time only in small spurts or when the score is lopsided. To complicate matters, parents look at their kid and compare her to the kids who are playing ahead of her. From the parents' perspective, there's no way that the youngster is not as good, if not better than, the other kids. That only adds to the friction. Then add in the reality that parents are driving their bench-warmer to faraway games and tournaments on the weekends, only to sit and watch other kids play and have fun. Parents are thinking about the expense of being on the team, the cost of room, board, and gas on the road, the time spent away from the rest of the family, and of course, the emotional expense that their child is going through.

This, of course, is a surefire formula for an angry confrontation between a frustrated parent and the coach. Even worse, the other parents of the bench-warmers will gradually tend to flock together; they'll commiserate about the unfairness of the situation, they'll vent their emotions to one another, and before too long, there'll be real resentment building toward the coach of the team:

- *How could he have the nerve to play his son the entire game at center and not give anybody else a chance to play there?*
- *Does this coach really think we drove three hours to get here, only to watch our daughter spend most of the game on the bench?*
- *I know the coach said only the better players would get the lion's share of playing time, but clearly my kid is better than the boy who is playing ahead of him. Why doesn't the coach give my son some real playing time so he can see for himself?*

As a parent of a travel team youngster, these are the kinds of situations you want to avoid at all costs. Teams become polarized, parents get angry, and the kids end up being the innocent victims. So how do you make sure your child doesn't fall into this kind of trap?

Again, have the courage to ask the right questions before your son or daughter makes that full commitment to the team. Have a mature conversation with the coach and ask him or her the following questions:

- *Coach, when you say that the better or more experienced players will get the most playing time, what's the minimum guarantee that every child will get?*

Listen very carefully to the coach's answer. Some travel coaches will say that it is impossible to predict just how much time every kid will get in every game, but that he'll do his best to get every kid in, depending on the game's circumstances. Other travel coaches will say that every youngster is guaranteed to play at least a quarter or a third of every game, and will often get more playing time than that.

• Ask yourself: *Which travel coach would you prefer that your son or daughter play for?*

Remember this: There are very few more disheartening experiences in a youngster's life than to sit on the bench and rarely get in. Or to get in only when the game's score is lopsided. No matter how much you try to boost a kid's sagging self-confidence with pep talks, unless he has a chance to go out and do his thing at some point, there's no upside to sitting on the bench for most of the game.

If you were to give a youngster the choice of being on a travel team but rarely having a chance to play in the game or being on the rec team and playing a lot in every game, chances are that your child will opt to play. Kids know that the real fun comes only from playing, not from sitting and watching.

There was a study done a few years ago on this very topic. A survey of kids ages five to twelve asked whether they would prefer to be a member of a championship team, but play very rarely, or be a member of an average team, but play a lot, in all of the games. Not surprisingly, *more than 90 percent of the kids polled said that they would much prefer to play on the average team so long as they played* rather than sit on the bench on the championship team.

    • *Coach, my youngster is involved in a number of extracurricular projects after school. I assume it's okay if she has to miss an occasional practice and game during the season?*

Again, listen carefully to what the coach has to say. Because of the length of the travel team season, most coaches will understand if your child misses practice or even a game every so often. More often than not, all the coach will ask for is a couple of weeks' notice, and in truth that's only fair.

However, be forewarned. Some travel coaches are very demanding about missed practices and games. They might even have a strict team policy about kids who miss practice being punished by being forced to sit out the first half of an upcoming game. In some cases, the coach may even decide to ask the youngster to leave the team! Again, be sure to know the coach's rules up front before the season gets under way, and just how lenient he or she is.

When Ryan was about to join his travel team, I made it a point to meet with his coach and inform him of a family vacation that we had already planned. This allowed the coach enough time to plan for Ryan's absence and nobody was caught off guard.

• *Coach, when can we get a copy of the practice and game schedule so that we can see if there are conflicts?*

This is just common sense, yet unfortunately too many parents—probably because they're thrilled that their child made the travel team—forget to ask about the schedule. For example, you may be under the impression that the travel coach is going to run practices from 4 to 6 p.m. on Tuesday and Thursday, because that's when he ran practices last year. That schedule works perfectly for you, because Joanie has a math tutorial class on Monday and Wednesday afternoons, and thus Tuesdays and Thursdays are open for her. But then, a week later, after you sign Joanie up for the team, you discover that the coach has changed the practice schedule this year to—yep!—Monday and Wednesday. Again, this is one of the basic questions to ask before your child makes the full commitment.

• *Coach, I just want to make sure that you have a little background on my son. His best position is point guard, and after years of watching him and coaching him myself, I can tell you that he's much more effective when he starts as opposed to coming off the bench.*

This may seem a little obvious to many parents, but when your kid opts to play for a travel team, chances are that the coach will place him in the position that the coach feels will best benefit the team. So if the coach thinks that your child can help the team win by being a forward instead of a guard, or by being the sixth man who comes off the bench in the middle of the game, then you, as the parent, have to accept this. That's not to say that you can't gently mention to the coach that your child has always played point guard, but be very careful about making any demands or putting any restrictions about where he has to play. That's really crossing the line between parent and coach.

Along that same line, unless your child has a serious medical or psychological issue that the coach should definitely be made aware of, you really don't have to caution the coach about your child's sensitivity or burning desire to play just one position. Don't worry: After a few practice sessions, the coach will quickly pick up on the unique traits of each youngster on the team. After all, that's what good coaches are supposed to do.

IF YOU DO HAPPEN TO HAVE A PROBLEM WITH THE TRAVEL TEAM COACH . . .

The same approach applies as with any other coach. Find a time when the coach is available, and has the ability to focus his or her attention on your concern. Most important, approach him or her with civility and with a sense of cooperation—*never* confrontation:

Coach, I was wondering if I could talk with you for a few moments about Eric's progress on the team so far. It's pretty obvious that he's not getting as much playing time as the other kids on the team, and I was wondering what the problem was. After all, let's face it, we're spending a lot of time and money for him to be on this team, plus we're traveling two or three hours to his away games. It's pretty depressing just to see him sit all the time on the bench. What are you going to do about it?

For many parents, this seems like a pretty reasonable approach. But if you were the coach, you probably would find yourself on the defensive. Indeed, some travel coaches will flat out remind you that, *Remember, in our first meeting, I promised no guarantees on playing time?*

In other words, you and the coach should be looking for a positive outcome—a solution—to the issue at hand, not a potential conflict that could escalate. There's no reason to complain that you're spending a lot of money for your child to be on this team, or that it's not right that you drive several hours to a game, only to see your boy sit on the bench. The coach is already well aware of this, and as soon as you bring it up, you're going to start transforming a civil conversation into a polarizing, defensive one in which the coach feels as though he or she has to defend his or her moves.

Perhaps a better approach might be:

Coach, I know that when we signed Eric up for the travel team, there were no guarantees made about playing time. But at this point in the season, it's becoming clear that he is not enjoying as much playing time as he would like. Is there something about his game that he can work on in practice so that he can get more time in the games? Or maybe there's another position he should play. Coach, playing on this team is very meaningful to my son, so he's hoping he can work to find a way to get past this issue.

The difference here is subtle but important. Rather than make the travel coach feel that he or she is somehow cheating your son, the parent here is asking the coach what they can do *together* to help Eric overcome this hurdle. It's clear that the parent is concerned, but it's also clear that the parent wants to work with the coach to help make Eric a better player. There's no guilt trip about how much money is being spent, or how much time is being devoted to all the travel.

Instead, the parent has said his or her piece in a matter of minutes, and if the coach is a reasonable person, then he or she will certainly make an effort to rectify the situation. All coaches know that every kid wants to play in the games, and play a lot. You don't have to remind the coach of that. But what this conversation has communicated is that your child has become frustrated, and now it's time for the coach to step in and try to help Eric find a way to overcome his frustrations.

This kind of communication works at the big-league level, too. In my career I played for nine different major league managers. Each spring, I made it a point to talk with the manager, just to make sure we both had similar expectations for me as a ballplayer. I found that to be extremely helpful as I went through my paces.

By the way, this travel team example just happens to concern an issue about playing time. If there are other issues you have with the coach—e.g., the coach's use of profanity, concerns about missing practices, etc.—you are still always better off thinking ahead of time what you want to say to the coach, so that the right tone is struck. Think about your words. Plan the time to speak to the coach. And then, when you do have your conversation, make it a pleasant one.

Unfortunately, too many travel team parents shoot right from the hip. They don't plan or choose their words carefully. They're angry and frustrated, and they approach the coach ready to vent. That only makes things worse, and usually the innocent victim in these kinds of situations is the young athlete. That's not fair to the child. Why should a child have to pay the price because an angry parent said something stupid to a coach?

WHAT IF YOUR KID GETS CUT?

One of the givens in any tryout situation is that every child goes in assuming that she has a good chance of making the travel team. Problem is, with travel teams, only a relatively small percentage of kids actually do make the cut. The question then is how, as a parent, do your cushion the blow when your child doesn't see his name on the travel team list?

By the time a child is, say, thirteen or fourteen, she has usually developed a certain level of emotional maturity and sophistication and can look around at the number of aspiring players and see for herself that it's going to be difficult to make the team. The thirteen-year-old immediately begins to sort through all of the kids who are competing for her position, and after a while, she has a pretty decent idea how she stacks up against her competitors. It's a self-comparison that all athletes go through, and believe it or not, by the time they're in the early teens, kids are usually pretty accurate in their analysis of their ability and their competitors' abilities. It's just part of the emotional maturity that grows with all adolescents.

As a result, when the list is posted, it usually isn't that much of a surprise for the thirteen-year-old to see who made the team and who didn't. If she didn't make the cut, she has already psychologically prepared herself for the fact that this might happen. Yes, of course, she hurts inside, but because of her age and ability to size up the competition, she is not usually shocked.

In contrast, a seven- or eight-year-old hasn't developed this psychological ability to look around at his competitors and see how he compares. For someone that young, it's just not part of his overall makeup yet. Even though there might be lots of kids trying out for only a handful of slots, and even though, as a good parent, you may have cautioned him about the odds against him, a kid that young really doesn't comprehend what you're saying.

As such, it can come as an unexpected blow when your eight-year-old doesn't see his name on the travel team list. Some kids just burst into tears. Others get extremely angry. Most, however, are so stunned that they don't even know how to react. They run to you in need of support.

In short, it's a heartbreaking scene all around. That's why I caution parents to be very, very careful about having their son or daughter try out for a travel team. You do have to sit your child down before the tryouts and explain carefully that not everyone makes the team. Even more important, have a backup plan in case your child doesn't make the squad (such as a local rec team). Also, remind your son or daughter that not making a travel team at seven or eight is not the end of the world, and certainly not the end of his or her competition in the sport. Many great athletes weren't really standout athletes when they were seven or eight, and if they had decided to quit sports when they faced adversity as a kid, then they would have never grown up to become stars.

I guess the overall point is that you want to prepare your child for what might happen, but in addition, you don't want any disappointment to prematurely end his or her involvement in sports. Sadly, too many kids get cut from a travel team at an early age and then decide to just give up sports entirely. Rather than trying out for another team, the kids are just so devastated that they walk away from the sport entirely. That's the worst possible outcome.

THE IMPORTANCE OF COPING WITH ADVERSITY

Understand this: There isn't an athlete alive who hasn't had to deal with a setback, disappointment, or unexpected turn of events in his or her sports career. I'm not talking about a defeat or a loss; I'm talking about getting cut from a team, or being told that you aren't good enough, or sitting on the bench, or even going through a rough stretch in which you begin to question your ability as an athlete.

Most coaches talk about the positives that come from playing sports, such as sportsmanship, team play, commitment to a goal, and so on. But to me, it's just as important that a youngster learns how to confront and grapple with adversity. No, it's not an easy lesson to learn, and for a parent, it can be gut-wrenching to see your child have to go through the process. But in the long run, for those kids who are able to work past that unexpected hurdle or bump in the road, the positive rewards are more than worth the struggle.

I can recall vividly when the Orioles started the 1988 season by going winless in our first twenty-one games. Can you imagine? We were 0–21! But instead of everyone panicking or giving up on one another, that very difficult start to the season actually brought the entire team closer together. We knew that if we were going to overcome this tough hurdle, we would have to do it together—as a team.

And we did. It was one of the great lessons I have learned from playing sports.

Once your child overcomes his roadblock, he will emerge with an even greater sense of self-confidence, and with the feeling that he can tackle all sorts of other problems. In my opinion, that's one of the major benefits of youth sports.

The sports world is filled with stories of athletes who didn't let adversity get in the way of their dreams. Jim Abbott was born without a right hand. That didn't stop him from becoming an outstanding high school, college, and major league pitcher. Michael Jordan got cut from his high school team when he was a sophomore. That didn't stop him, either. When Steve Young, the NFL Hall of Famer, got to Brigham Young University as a freshman, he was listed as number 8 on the quarterback depth chart. That's right—there were seven quarterbacks listed ahead of him. Steve was so low on the charts that he called his parents back in Connecticut and told them he was ready to come home. Fortunately for BYU and NFL fans everywhere, Steve's parents comforted him, but also insisted that he stay at BYU and work through his adversity.

The point is, if your child is going to play competitive sports, then you have to be there to support her. That means you have to be there for her to celebrate the good days, but even more important, you have to be there for her when things aren't going so well. It's easy to be a sports parent when your kid hits a home run; it's not easy

Travel Team Injuries Rise

For the last decade, more and more doctors have seen a major increase in the number of kids who get hurt playing sports, especially those kids who play on elite travel teams.

Now two top sports physicians in Washington State have found in separate studies that kids who compete at elite levels of youth sports significantly increase their risk of being injured. The studies determined that only 6 percent of fifth-grade travel team soccer players in the Puget Sound area suffered injuries, but that those numbers rose significantly over time. By the time the travel team soccer players were in eighth grade, 40 percent of the players reported serious injuries.

Remember: The dramatic increase in games and practices can make kids more susceptible to injury.

when she strikes out three times in a game, or when she doesn't make the travel team.

WHAT YOU SHOULD SAY AND DO

So what do you say to your youngster if he doesn't make the cut? For starters, give him a big, long hug. As grown-ups, we already know that life is full of ups and downs, and that we try to maximize the good days and minimize the bad ones. But that's from the perspective of an adult. When you're only eight or ten or twelve years old, the world is still new. Not making the travel team can be devastating to a youngster, especially if she sees that some friends did make the squad.

No matter how much travel coaches caution parents and their kids that "making this team is going to be very, very tough," invariably those words just don't sink in. Or if the kid and the parent do hear these words, their quiet reaction is something along the lines of, *Yeah, but I'm sure we'll make it.*

Unfortunately, when that list is posted and the youngster's name isn't on it, all sorts of havoc can be unleashed. That's because not only is the child disappointed, but many times the parent's disappointment boils over into anger—anger at the coach and the evaluators. Ugly confrontations can occur. Sometimes, even violence.

Because of all these negative situations, it's smart for any parent to sit down with a seven- or eight-year-old and discuss the realities of trying out for a travel team. The last thing you want to do is set your child up for a bitter disappointment so early in her life. And there's plenty of evidence that when a child goes out for a travel team and gets cut, that youngster just won't go out for that sport ever again. In effect, he's become a "has been" at the tender age of eight.

The reasons are clear and easy to understand from the child's point of view. No child wants to go through the embarrassment and humiliation of trying out again, only to get cut again. *Besides,* most kids will say, *What chance do I have of making the team next year? All the kids on the team this season will be that much better because they have played at a higher level than I have. Plus all the coaches will know them— and they won't know me.*

This all places the parent in a very awkward spot. On one hand, you want to sincerely encourage your child not to give up on her dream, that if she works hard at her skills, then next year she'll be better than the kids on this year's travel team. But on the other hand, the cold hard truth is that, with many travel teams, once a kid doesn't make the team, it does become that much more difficult to make the squad the following year. By then, friendships have been formed among the travel coaches, the players, and their parents, and the coaches will be very reluctant to cut a "veteran" travel team player to make room for a "rookie."

So what do you do? If you, in your wisdom as a parent, feel that there's a decent chance that your child might not make the travel team, you might want to minimize the importance of that team, and instead just focus on finding a club where your child will be able to get lots of playing time. Again, I can't overemphasize the importance of building up self-confidence in youth sports, and the only way to do that is for them to get lots of playing time.

WHAT ABOUT KIDS WHO PLAY INDIVIDUAL SPORTS?

There may not be travel teams for kids who play individual sports, but there's still a hefty amount of competition that begins to set in at early ages. Kids who compete in tennis, golf, figure skating, gymnastics, track, and other singular sports find out very quickly that competitions are a major part of these sports. Even at ages seven or eight, individual scores and judging marks start to be kept by judges, and the kids (and their parents) can begin to see how they stack up against their competitors.

For parents of individual-sport athletes, this can be even more nerve-racking than watching kids play a team sport. That's because in a soccer or baseball game, an individual player can still do well even if the team does poorly. For example, if your son gets three hits in the game, but his baseball team loses 8–2, he still feels pretty good about his performance.

But in tennis, if your son goes out and loses 6–0 and 6–1 to an opponent, then it's pretty hard for him to hide his disappointment. Kids who play individual sports learn early on in life that their winning or losing is on their own shoulders. As you might imagine, that can be a difficult and sometimes harsh lesson to learn at a young age.

DEALING WITH "ALIBI IKES"

Sometimes, kids may have a difficult time taking responsibility for losing in a competition, and they will begin to develop psychological defense mechanisms to protect their young and fragile egos. In other words, they will make excuses for their less than stellar performances:

- *The judges clearly favored the other girl. That's why she won and not me.*
- *My opponent was cheating. He called my shots out when they were definitely in. That's why I lost.*
- *I don't know why I didn't run better today. I think it was because my lower back has been hurting.*

Kids will very often try to come up with some sort of alibi that, at least in their minds, will excuse them from a less than victorious performance. It's almost as though they can't find it within themselves to acknowledge that one of their opponents clearly had a better day, or they don't want to acknowledge that they might not be as good or as talented as their opponent. This is, of course, all part of sportsmanship, and why a certain level of emotional maturity is required before any youngster can fully understand what it means to be a good sport.

If your child shows some indications of being an "Alibi Ike," give him plenty of room at first to express his feelings. After all, he is young, and youngsters will look for reasons (even imaginary ones) as to why they didn't win or play better. But then, as he progresses through the season, you should find some time to gently and patiently tell him that it's okay to lose as long as you do your best—and that furthermore, there's nothing wrong with saluting one's opponent for having a good day. In fact, that's the essence of sportsmanship, and that's a lesson he'll need to learn if he wants to keep competing in his sport.

Don't expect just one lesson about not making excuses to sink in. The reality is that you're going to have to remind your youngster whenever she is reaching for excuses that such statements are frowned upon. Tell your child that she will be held in higher regard if she can somehow move past feeling cheated out of winning by acknowledging how well her opponent played. Reinforce that lesson as best you can.

One other note: Always avoid the lecture! If there's one thing that all kids hate, it's the "sports lecture" from Mom or Dad. If you feel that you have something to say to your daughter about any issue in her game, whether it be sportsmanship, making excuses, or how to improve her game, just make sure your advice is clear, right to the point, and delivered in less than a minute. You may feel that you want to go on and talk more about this issue, but trust me—kids will listen to about thirty to forty seconds before their minds begin to wander on to something else. Make your point succinctly and then move on. And don't worry—your child will get the point.

HOW CAN I TELL IF MY CHILD IS GOING TO BE A STAR IN AN INDIVIDUAL SPORT?

One of the real difficulties with individual sports like gymnastics, figure skating, swimming, and tennis is that they culminate with the youngster reaching his peak at fifteen or sixteen years old. As a parent, how do you know when your child is eight or ten whether she really does have a chance to become the next Sarah Hughes or Andre Agassi? After all, if she does seem to have that kind of unique star ability, shouldn't you start looking at stepping up her practice sessions?

Here's a suggestion. Since it's so hard to predict how any ten-year-old is going to progress, rather than using your own judgment, look around in your community and see if you can find two or three experts in your child's sport to offer their own personal evaluations. Let's say, for example, that your nine-year-old daughter is a gymnast. Before you sign her up for extensive lessons and practice time, you might want to first find a gymnastics coach from a local university or AAU team to come and take a look at your child. Let the coach guide you as to whether your daughter will have what it takes to go to the next level in competitive gymnastics. In other words, don't rely on your own evaluation—get some input from other folks who aren't so emotionally tied to your child's success. Once you have gathered all that information, you can then better figure out the next step for your child. But again, do your homework first and by all means make sure your child has the interest and desire to take her efforts to the next level!

Key Chapter Takeaways

1. Before you sign your child up for a travel team tryout, be sure to do your homework well in advance. Travel team experiences can be very unpredictable.

2. Kids care more about getting to play in the game than anything else. So if a local rec team will meet their needs, a travel team may not be necessary.

3. Conflicts with travel team coaches should be handled in a civilized way, just as with any other coach. Avoid an angry confrontation and steer clear of any disgruntled factions of parents that may develop.

Chapter 7

THE MIDDLE SCHOOL YEARS (AGES 12–14)

During middle school, our young children transition into their preteen and teenage years. It's a time of magical change for all kids, especially those kids who play sports.

We know from our own experiences that all sorts of hormonal and psychological changes happened when we advanced from fifth and sixth grade into seventh and eighth. For example, some of the kids who grew early on leveled off; other youngsters started to go through a growth spurt. Some kids who had a roll or two of baby fat grew into lean and trim hard-bodies. Other youngsters, who seemed all floppy, with outsized feet, started to grow into themselves and become fine and sturdy athletes.

I can see that with Ryan. He has good size now as a sixth-grader (five-five and 110 pounds), but you can tell that he's going to continue to go on growing later, like I did. He's still in what I call a "puppy" stage, with big floppy feet. Some of his friends, though, have gone through a more accelerated pace into adolescence and they're the shining stars on the ball field right now. But I was a late bloomer, and my wife Kelly is six feet tall herself, so there's every indication that Ryan is a long way from reaching his full height. That was true with Rachel as well. She's now a sophomore in high school and she's five-eleven.

There are many obvious changes during the preteen years. Kids start to wear braces on their teeth. The boys find their voices beginning to deepen, and maybe even start to develop some peach fuzz on their faces. But there are other much more subtle changes occurring as well. By the time many kids reach the seventh grade, a good portion of them—and many of them outstanding and gifted athletes— will start exploring other avenues in life, and will start to pursue other dreams far away from the playing field. Some of these youngsters will find their true calling in the theater and in school plays; some will be drawn to serious scientific research; others still will find that they truly enjoy developing new software on their computers. Whatever their calling may be, you as an adult have to understand that this is all very natural and part of the typical maturation process. Your child may be one of those kids who discovers on her own that playing sports is no longer the biggest attraction or driving force in her life.

This is an important lesson to learn, because it reinforces one of the basic principles about parenting kids in sports: *You must always remember that it's not about your dreams in sports—it's about your child's dreams.* And if it turns out that your son or daughter finds something else in life more exciting than shooting baskets or turning double plays, it's essential that you, as the parent and resident grown-up, understand this reality, accept it, and then give just as much support as you possibly can.

We've all heard about parents who live vicariously through their children. Well, that's exactly what I'm talking about. It's wonderful and joyous if your child has developed the same kind of passion for a sport that you had as a youngster, but just in case she hasn't, be sure that you don't push her to pursue a dream that is really more yours than hers.

LET YOUR MIDDLE SCHOOLER LEARN "CONCEPTS"

Entering middle school is also the right age to start emphasizing concepts in sports. That is, if a young athlete is ever going to absorb the intricacies and finer points of his game, this is the time. During these middle school years, kids have to learn how to advance their game by trying, testing, and trusting their own instincts. Too many youth coaches today dictate exactly what they want athletes to do in every situation, on every play, so that kids are merely following orders, and not really grasping the concepts of the game. Whether it's learning how to run the bases on their own, or figuring out which base to throw to, or calling their own game when they're pitching, you have to let kids learn these basics of the game. Remember, at this level, it's supposed to be a learning experience for kids, not just learning to do what the coach tells them to do. Let kids use their own eyes and instincts—let them respond to what they see for themselves on the field.

I think that coaches try to protect kids too much. That's why in big games and tournaments, they'll start calling pitches and telling kids when to tag up. Coaches will rationalize: *Well, if the kid gives up a big hit and we end up losing, I can at least go to the pitcher and say, "It's my fault, not yours. I called the wrong pitch."* Coaches feel that they can protect kids like that, especially kids who they think aren't very good at handling disappointment. I totally understand that perspective and appreciate the sensitivity to the youngsters' feelings, but I have to disagree. I think making bad plays or poor judgments when you're a kid is part of the learning experience in sports. Yes, it may be painful when it happens, but it teaches you how to learn from that experience.

Don't forget—adversity usually teaches a young athlete well. Failure is a major part of any sport. A youngster's ability to deal with it is critically important to her overall development. You can only do so much as a coach or as a parent. You have to let kids go out and play up to their own abilities. You can't play the games for them. You can calm them down afterward and support them. But, ironically, the more detailed instruction you give them during the game, the more you're probably getting in the way of their progress. All of this extra coaching takes away from a kid's development. How is a kid going to learn the instincts for the game if every one of his plays is pre-decided for him by his coach?

PACK TWO PARACHUTES IN LIFE

When Grant Hill, the great NBA basketball player, was growing up, he was told by his parents, Calvin and Janet Hill, that while it was great to have the dream of someday playing basketball in the pro ranks, he needed to have another dream in life just in case that first one didn't come true. Calvin, who starred as a running back at Yale and then became a top running back in the NFL, knew from firsthand experience about having a backup plan in life— a second parachute in case the first one doesn't open. In his own career, Calvin had seen scores of top athletes who, due to either injury or unfortunate circumstances, had their careers cut short. That's why Calvin and Janet cautioned their son at an early age to be sure to develop another passion, or goal, in his life just in case the basketball dream didn't come true.

Grant was smart enough to heed his parents' words. So, as a youngster growing up in suburban Virginia, in addition to pursuing basketball, Grant studied hard in school and of course eventually graduated from Duke University, one of the top schools in the country. His high school and college education became his backup parachute, and it's clearly worked well for him. Grant's dream came true. He was a star at Duke University and made it to the NBA, but as most basketball fans know, he has had a string of injuries during his career. In my case, when I was drafted by the Orioles out of high school, they guaranteed that they would pay my college tuition if I decided to attend. That promise from Baltimore served as my backup parachute.

It's during the middle school years that you should begin to impress upon your child the importance of having two parachutes in life. By the time she's in sixth, seventh, or eighth grade, start to emphasize to her how important it is to develop another interest or passion in life, just in case the sports dream doesn't come true. It doesn't matter what other interests your child develops, so long as he finds something that is positive and meaningful to him, and best of all, serves as a true backup in case his sports career doesn't take him beyond middle school or high school.

Remember, less than 5 percent of all high school varsity athletes ever go on to play sports in college, so the numbers suggest that it's prudent to have your youngster develop other interests. Last year, the NCAA ran some very smart advertisements on television, in which the point was that there are literally hundreds of thousands of college

The Odds of Getting a Scholarship

According to the *San Jose Mercury News,* in 2004 there were 360,000 athletes at the Division I, II, and III levels of college. Of those, only about 126,000 received some form of athletic scholarship aid. That's a pretty impressive number, until you realize that there are close to 41 million below-college-age kids who play sports in this country.

Here's another thought: NCAA colleges offer about $1 billion in athletic scholarships, but there's more than $22 billion in academic scholarships available to students who want to go to college.

students-athletes who are going to turn pro—but they're going to turn pro in some other career besides sports.

THE LESSON OF BALANCING ONE'S TIME

As young athletes progress into the middle school years, the number of hours in the day will seem to shrink. As kids continue to climb the ladder in sports, you can expect that their practice and game schedules will begin to lengthen and expand. Especially if your child is playing on a travel team, you can now expect that she will have practice at least twice weekly after school, and usually a game on both Saturday and Sunday. And with most travel teams, holiday weekends, such as Labor Day, Thanksgiving, Presidents'

Day, Martin Luther King Day, and the Christmas and Easter breaks, will most likely bring more games as well. As a parent, you have to be well aware of this kind of time and travel commitment before your child signs up.

On a daily basis, your child's life is going to be quite full. Every hour is going to be accounted for. Assuming practice is either right after school or, sometimes, during the evening hours, it's important that you begin to teach your son or daughter about how to balance schoolwork with an athletic schedule. Don't assume that your child will naturally or instinctively know how to do this! Rather, as you approach the school year, take some time to go over his study habits so he can maximize his efforts with school and with sports. For example, if you take your child out to purchase school supplies for the upcoming year, that's a good time to talk about time management. Perhaps you can buy her a small notebook, so that she can write down her homework assignments each day. Explain to her that if she wants to play a travel sport, then she has to understand that there are going to be days (and nights) when she comes home dog tired from practice and homework is still looming. She can't say, *Mom, can't I just shower and go to bed?*

Let your child know that the homework always comes first, and that if he begins to fall behind in his studies or with his grades, then the sports will be benched. Set the priority up front and repeat it often. Let him know that playing sports is a privilege—not a right—and that he will only be given that privilege if his grades are up to your expectations. This is an excellent time to talk about packing two parachutes as well.

Let your athlete know that learning how to balance her education with her athletics is a life lesson that will serve her well. There are all sorts of studies that suggest that athletes who learn how to balance academics with sports not only end up with better grades, but they also build better self-confidence, are more well-rounded in their interests, and become prepared for life's challenges after their school and sports years are completed. So, from a parenting perspective, this conversation with your middle-schooler is a vital one, and one that should happen before the school year gets going.

So how does a youngster learn this lesson? Sit down with him and show him how many open hours he has after school every day. If school ends at, say, 3 p.m., and he has soccer practice at 5, then explain to him how to come home and hit the books from 3:30 to 4:30. During that time, he can have a worthwhile snack, and at 4:30 he can start getting ready for soccer practice. Then, when he returns home, he can shower, have dinner, and then study again until all of the homework is completed. If it is completed by nine, then he can watch a favorite program on television, or chat with his friends on the telephone or online.

The sooner you can impress your child with this daily regimen, the sooner she will become comfortable with it, and will actually look forward to it. Too many kids have unstructured lives. They'll come home from school, watch television for a couple of hours, eat something, and then go to soccer practice. By the time they get home again, they eat dinner, and then will have to stay up to eleven to finish all of their homework. By then, they're exhausted, you're exhausted, and they're angry that they missed their favorite show, and of course, angry that they couldn't chat with their friends. Even worse, sometimes, they'll be so tired that they won't finish all of their homework or preparation for tomorrow's test.

PLAY ON MORE THAN ONE TEAM?
WHAT ABOUT COMMITMENT?

During the middle school years, there are still lots of kids who don't want to choose between two sports that occur during the same season. For example, what do you do when your child wants to continue to play both basketball and ice hockey? Since both sports are played primarily during the winter months, trying to juggle schedules in both can become a full-time job for any parent. It can also cause even more complications, not only with time management, but also with the child's commitment to each team.

No parent wants to find him or herself in the position of having to tell a youngster, *No, you can't play both sports,* but in truth, by the time your youngster is eleven or twelve or older, you can certainly sit down and explain to him the realities of the situation: *Josh, I know you love both basketball and ice hockey, but I just looked at the team schedules for this coming winter season, and both teams practice at the same time on Tuesday and Thursday evenings. Even worse, both teams play a lot of games on Saturdays and Sundays. That means if you try to play for both teams, you'll end up missing practices and games all over the place. And you may end up losing out on both teams.*

The typical athletic twelve-year-old is going to ask immediately: *But why can't I try to play on both teams? Won't the coaches understand that if I happen to miss an occasional basketball practice, it's only because I'm playing hockey? Besides, playing two sports will keep me in great shape!*

This discussion will invariably lead to the question of commitment. According to most sports-parenting experts and youth coaches, by the time a youngster has reached middle school, the concept of "commitment to one's team" will have jumped up several rungs on the priority ladder. So, when your middle-schooler starts asking why she can't play on both teams simultaneously, this is the time to reintroduce the idea of commitment. You have to paint a clear and complete picture ahead of time, so that your child fully understands what it means to commit to a team. (By the way, you also have to explain to her that regardless of whether she is the star or sits on the bench, she has to stay on the team.)

But I'll only miss a few practices and games during the season, your youngster will complain. This is when you explain that to miss games and practices because you belong to another team is not only not fair to all the other kids on the team, but also downright selfish. In effect, the young athlete is putting her personal needs and desires ahead of all the other kids.

If the youngster still doesn't accept your explanation, try this approach: *Josh, suppose you were on the same basketball team with your friend Mike. Mike's a terrific athlete; in fact, in addition to playing on the basketball team with you, he also plays during the winter season on a travel hockey team. But as a result of being on both teams, there are a lot of conflicts with the schedules. As a result, Mike misses a lot of basketball practices but still very much expects to play a lot in the games. So, let me ask you this: How would you like it if, on game day, Mike came to the basketball game and he ended up playing a lot more in the game than you did? Would that seem fair to you? Or would you be angry that a teammate who doesn't come to all the practices ends up getting more time in the games than you do?*

Perhaps once you put it in that light, your youngster will gain a better understanding of how commitment to only one team is a key part of his development. It's a lesson that he might not agree with at first, but ultimately, it's a lesson of fairness for all kids who play sports. The bottom line? See if your child can choose one sport over another and commit to it for a season.

SPECIALIZATION: WHEN SHOULD KIDS DECIDE ON A SPORT?

Right around this time in their development, lots of kids will begin to realize that if they really want to progress to a higher level in sports, it may be worth their while to simply specialize in one athletic activity. The question is then: Which one?

To me, there's still a huge value in learning and playing other sports. When I was a kid, you instinctively knew when to move from one sport to the next according to the season. Take football, for example. We played a lot of football, and I loved it and I was very good at it. When baseball season ended in the fall, I picked up a football and played with Billy and our friends.

I have a couple of strong opinions on specialization. When you're developing athletically, other sports will challenge you as well. In soccer, for example, you're developing skills with your feet. In basketball, your movements are explosive and quick. Baseball will challenge you in many other ways athletically. Overall, I tell kids: *Don't specialize— if you're good enough, play as many sports as you can.* Over time, however, your child may begin to develop his or her own choice of a particular sport. And by the way, that decision comes from the kid, not the parent.

Kids very often do decide to specialize in one sport or two by the time they're in middle school, around the age of thirteen. Such a decision is a highly individualized one, and it should be according to each youngster's own needs and desires. There is no one hard and fast rule, but there are some general guidelines to bear in mind.

There's some mythology involved in the idea that deciding to specialize in just one sport at a relatively early age will truly propel an athlete to become a superstar by the time she's in high school. In my opinion, that's simply not a guarantee you or your child should ever rely on.

Let me be more specific: Let's assume your daughter is a fine soccer player. From the very first time she stepped foot on a soccer field when she was five or six, it was clear that she had an instinctive feel for the game and how to excel at it. But in addition to soccer, she was such a well-rounded and natural athlete that she also excelled immediately in basketball, softball, lacrosse, and tennis. In fact, pretty much any sporting activity she tried, she immediately did well in. During her elementary school years, she played a variety of these sports, and she changed sports according to the season.

But now that she's in sixth grade, more and more of her original soccer-playing teammates have decided that in order to keep progressing in that sport, they will play on a local travel team. That team plays a rigorous schedule starting right after Labor Day and goes through the fall, through the winter indoors, and then into the spring season. The idea, of course, is that by specializing and focusing all of their athletic energies into just soccer, these girls will immediately place themselves on the fast track to develop their skills, gain more experience, and play only against top-flight competition. On the downside, these girls have pretty much decided by age eleven or twelve that soccer is definitely going to be their primary sport.

Yes, they may dabble in some other school intramural sports, but clearly their full-time commitment is to soccer.

So now your daughter finds herself at a crossroads. Does she follow her friends and commit herself only to the travel team in soccer? Or does she continue to play soccer in the fall, basketball in the winter, and softball in the spring? And if she does maintain a three-sport career, is she accidentally short-circuiting her soccer plans by not specializing in that sport? Will she ever be able to catch up with her soccer-playing friends?

This is a most difficult question for today's athletes and their parents to ponder. A generation ago, the sports seasons were so well defined that no one had to face this kind of dilemma: you merely played the sport you wanted to according to the school calendar. But as travel teams have proliferated and the competition has increased dramatically, kids are being faced with this question of specialization at a much earlier age.

As noted, there is no one clear-cut rule about what's right and wrong here. But if you look at the specialization from the perspective of college coaches who do a lot of recruiting, they will almost universally tell you that they look first for the well-rounded athlete—the youngster who didn't feel the need to specialize in just one sport at an early age. College coaches often worry about a couple of things with the specialized athlete: one, that by the time he reaches college he might be running a risk of injury due to repetitive overuse of the same muscles and joints from a very early age, and two, psychologically, he also runs a greater risk of burning out. College coaches also instinctively recognize that kids who have the athletic ability to play a variety of sports in middle school and high school are probably fairly gifted athletes, and most college coaches want to have gifted athletes on their teams.

Again, this is just anecdotal observation from college coaches, and you and your child should do what you feel is best. But if your child tells you that she equally enjoys playing soccer, basketball, and lacrosse, then there certainly is no reason to press her into just one activity at an early age. By the time she gets to be fourteen or fifteen and in high school, she may have to choose only one or two sports in order to make a junior varsity or varsity team anyway. Or your child may discover along the way that he really does prefer to play only one sport. But whatever choice is made, the ultimate decision should always come from your child—not from you. That's not to say you can't provide some insight, but in the end, it's still your child's life, your child's athletic career, and your child's dreams, and as such, it's still your child's decision. That's all part of growing up.

To help in the decision-making process, you might ask your youngster to ask him or herself two basic questions:

1. *Of all the sports I play, which one is my favorite?*
2. *And what sport am I truly the best at?*

If the answer to both questions is the same, then there's usually no issue. But sometimes, there are two different responses (*I really love baseball . . . but in truth, my best sport is lacrosse*). Here again, you can provide some insight and assistance, but you want your youngster to make the ultimate decision for him- or herself.

Specialization at Too Young an Age: Be Careful!

Noted orthopedic surgeons everywhere have witnessed a dramatic rise in repetitive-use injuries in youngsters all over the country. What's particularly alarming to these specialists is that the kids needing surgery are getting younger and younger. And all of the doctors point to kids who are doing too much too soon in terms of their athletic careers.

Famed sports surgeon Dr. James Andrews recently told *The New York Times:* "You get a kid on the operating table and you say to yourself, 'It's impossible for a thirteen-year-old to have this kind of wear and tear.' We've got an epidemic going on."

Reports Dr. Scott Sigman, an orthopedic surgeon from Lowell, Massachusetts: "Some ten-year-olds are four-foot-two. Some are five-foot-two. The stress and strains on each body are very different. Sixteen seems to be the leveling-off point—that's the age at which each competitor's body has similarly matured, making high-intensity competition safer."

IS THE THREE-SPORT STAR REALLY GONE?

Unlike a generation ago, there are very few high school athletes who play three sports these days. Inevitably, somewhere along the way in middle school, they decided for themselves that they love several sports, but that they really love baseball or basketball or whatever. As a result, they make that one sport their top commitment, and as mentioned, they will sometimes play the other sports on a local rec or intramural team.

But back to the original question: *Will it hurt or slow down your child's athletic progress if she decides to keep playing a variety of sports in middle school rather than just specializing in one?* Just keep this in mind: From my perspective, it really makes no difference what sports your child plays when he's ten, because invariably the skills he develops from one sport will quickly translate into skills for another sport. For example, the foot speed and quickness that your daughter develops from playing hard-nosed defense in basketball will also help her foot speed and quickness in soccer or softball. The wrist strength that your son builds from shooting pucks in hockey will also translate into strengthening his wrists for swinging a baseball bat. You get the idea. Athletic skills and drills are not built in isolation. They will benefit the sport in season, and they will also benefit all the other sports that your child decides to play.

What's the bottom line? First, listen to your child and respect her desires and instincts. Let her tell you what she'd like to do. Second, reassure your child that there is no guarantee that either pathway is going to ensure that he'll be a star by the time he's in high school. Because so few kids ever go beyond high school varsity, it's really much more important that they play a sport that they truly love and have fun with. Ultimately, that's what counts.

So, try this approach. Why not ask your child which sport would provide him or her with the most fun? Remember, isn't that the reason kids are supposed to play sports in the first place?

ADDING MORE GAMES MAY NOT BE THE ANSWER

I've had a glove and a bat in my hands since I can remember. But my dad wasn't there giving me instruction every day. My brothers, Billy and Fred, and I just played. I was pretty good when I was eight or nine, better than a lot of kids my age, but I didn't have much size. A lot of kids could throw harder than I could. There were a lot of kids who could hit the ball farther than I could. But overall, I was still a pretty good ballplayer.

I started playing on an organized baseball team when I was eight. I was on the Angels. We played a total of eight games. Then the next two years I played on the Indians, and we played a total of nine to ten games. That was it for our season. The rest of the time Billy and I played our own pickup games with other kids in the neighborhood.

That's a far cry from many youth baseball leagues to-day, which include as many as fifty or sixty games in one spring and summer, and sometimes even more. I don't know if playing sixty games a season is such a great idea for kids, simply because I know that young ballplayers will sometimes get bored during the course of a long season, but I do know that most youth leagues like to add as many games to their schedule as possible.

My son played a lengthy schedule of more than sixty games for the first time this past summer, when he was eleven. I certainly had my concerns but it was something that he really wanted to do. After speaking with his coach several times to get a better understanding of his coaching philosophy, Kelly and I agreed to let Ryan play.

Ryan's coach believed that more and more games are scheduled simply because kids today don't go out on their own and play pickup games as we did when we were growing up. As a result, the only way that youngsters can truly im-prove and hone their skills is by having more scheduled games to play in. I certainly appreciate that approach but I do wish there were more pickup games like when we were kids. My sense is that an organized game structure doesn't allow kids to experiment with different approaches; that is, youngsters might want to try switch-hitting, or maybe try out a different position than the one they normally play, or change their batting stance or the way they pitch a ball. These kinds of "experiments" aren't really encouraged dur-ing the course of a formal game, and I think the kids miss out. Not only does this kind of experimentation tend to be great fun for the kids, but it also allows them to be, well, kids.

I have heard that in Europe, where most young athletes play on local club teams in their hometowns, there is a much different approach to practices and games. For example, here in the United States, a youth team might have only a handful of practices early in the season, and then play dozens of real games. In Europe, the coaches emphasize the practice sessions much more than the games. That is, for every three practice sessions, they will then have a game. Their philosophy is that by giving the kids more practice time, they have a much better chance of developing their skills and also have the opportunity to experiment with their approach to the game. That practice-to-game ratio of three to one makes a lot of sense to me as well. It could be baseball, basketball, hockey, you name it—every coach will tell you that the more you practice, the better you will become.

I understand that the games have more drama to them and that parents in particular prefer watching games as opposed to observing practice sessions. But in truth game situations tend to restrict kids in their sports. Because the youngsters don't want to make a mistake in a real game, they become much more tentative in their play: They're less likely to try something new because they're fearful that they may fail and thus risk the reprimands of their coach and even their mom or dad. Conversations like this happen all the time after games:

DAD: John, why did you try and stretch that single
into a double?

SON: I dunno, Dad . . . I just thought it would be fun
to see if I could run fast all the way to second and
surprise the outfielder and beat the throw.

DAD: Well, it wasn't a good play. You were out by at
least five feet.

What's the chance of that youngster trying to stretch
a single into a double ever again? Pretty much zero. But
my point is, how else in the world would this young
ballplayer ever develop his skills at running the bases unless he has the chance to go out and experiment and push
his limits every so often?

Perhaps having more practice sessions is the answer.
Finding a balance between trying new things in practice
and then trying them out in a game is a wonderful way to
allow a youngster to polish her skills on her own without
risking the wrath of her coach or parents.

WILL MORE PRACTICE GET THEM A
SCHOLARSHIP OR PRO CONTRACT?

Yes and no.

Yes—in the sense that in order to reach the pinnacle of
sports these days—which means getting a college athletic
scholarship or perhaps even a pro contract—any athlete is
going to have to have that inner drive within himself to go

out and practice and practice and practice some more. The world of athletics is just too vast and too competitive to think that your child's innate talent alone is going to be enough to get her into that rarefied elite fraternity of college or pro sports. So yes, if your kid truly wants to see just how far his God-given talent will take him, he's going to have to spend a lot of quality time practicing his skills.

That brings us to the second answer—and that is no. *Ironically, just because your kid works hard and wants to succeed doesn't mean that he was born with the innate talent to ever play in college or in the pros.*

Parents, let me be very clear about this—just because your youngster goes out and practices his sport fanatically *does not* guarantee that he will ever reach the top of the athletic pyramid. What all that hard work *will* guarantee, however, is that your child will reach a level in sport as high as his God-given potential will allow.

In other words, let's say your son is a baseball pitcher. He loves the sport—he eats, sleeps, and works at his craft every day: plays on not one but perhaps two youth baseball teams; works with a private pitching coach to help with his mechanics; goes to a specialized baseball camp in the summer where he can further work on his skills. In short, he's firing on all of his cylinders to become the very best pitcher he can be.

But if, at the end of all his hard work and dedicated practice, his potential is only good enough to make him an average pitcher on his high school baseball team, then the odds of him advancing to obtain a college baseball scholarship or a pro contract are pretty remote. That is, he's reached his full, God-given athletic potential. His peak is to throw a fastball 82 mph, and he also has a slow curve as a strikeout pitcher. That's certainly fine, and hopefully the youngster is pleased and satisfied that he's worked hard and achieved this level of athletic ability.

But the one essential key that he doesn't have—and that more practice won't bring him—is that God-given ability to have a major league arm. That's what too many sports parents fail to understand about getting to the next level in sports. Hard work and dedication are absolutely wonderful traits, but the most important trait is just God-given talent. And there's no way in the world that any parent can guarantee that for his or her child. The truth is, unless your youngster was born with that extraordinary ability, no amount of practice is going to propel her to become a superstar in college or in the pros.

That may be a cold, harsh reality for a lot of moms and dads to accept, but again, it's the truth. As such, you should encourage your child to work hard so that he can reach his potential in sports—but not necessarily so that he can achieve a college scholarship or a pro contract. Understand that if you're focusing on scholarships or pro sports, then inevitably, you're setting your child up for a major disappointment as she finishes her high school career. Remember, the numbers don't lie. Less than 5 percent of all high school varsity athletes ever go on to play sports in college.

The College Jump:
The Odds for High School Athletes

There are about 375,000 NCAA players in Divisions I, II, and III. Of that number, approximately 126,000 received partial or full athletic scholarships.

Of more than 900,000 high school football players, less than 6 percent will earn a spot on an NCAA football roster. And of the players who are good enough to play college ball, only about 2 percent of them will be drafted by the NFL.

With basketball, about 2.9 percent of all high school varsity basketball players will ever wear a college jersey. And of all the college players, about 1.3 percent will be good enough to be drafted by the NBA.

HOW IMPORTANT IS MAKING THE ALL-STAR TEAM?

It's a wonderful feeling for any young boy or girl to be selected by either a coach or by the child's peers for the all-star team, or to be selected to serve as the team captain. Not only does this kind of special honor add another layer of self-confidence, but it clearly is a nice milestone that suggests the child is doing well in sports, either because of talent, leadership, hard work, or best yet, a combination of all three.

As the parent of a middle school child, you should show your enthusiasm for such an achievement, and help your child celebrate the moment. (In fact, if you haven't started a scrapbook for your youngster, now's a good time to do so.) Let the moment sink in, and let your child enjoy his accomplishment.

But what happens if your child isn't fortunate enough to make the all-star team or be named captain? Is that a less-than-subtle message to your child that she isn't as athletically gifted as some of her peers? Or that maybe she should give up?

Absolutely not! There is no direct correlation between who the star athletes are at age twelve and who the star performers will be five or six years later, when they are juniors or seniors in high school. There are no long-term studies that I know of that show or substantiate the theory that the kids who are stars in middle school will also be stars by the time they graduate from high school.

Besides, common sense dictates that too many variables come into play for all youngsters. When they start growing into adolescence, the physical and psychological factors all kick in, and your little boy or girl is quickly growing into his or her own person. As a parent, you would like your youngster to continue competing with the same dedication and desire at the next level of sports, but the truth is that some kids—even some kids who make the all-star team—decide on their own that they've had enough of athletic competition and they drift into some other activity. Other kids who have shown just a middling interest in sports suddenly become enthralled with the essence of athletic competition and they can't wait to practice their game. Indeed, their desire to work out with their buddies and on their own will drive them to even greater heights. This helps explain why so many of our top athletes today were only so-so in terms of athletic talent when they were ten or twelve. In other words, they didn't make the all-star team or become the team captain. In fact, many of these stars of today were either playing different sports as kids, or they weren't playing sports at all. In addition, even if your child is an average athlete, the benefits that he will derive from sports are immeasurable.

Are Today's Youth Stars Also the Stars of Tomorrow?

In 1982, twelve-year-old Cody Webster of Kirkland, Washington, was considered a national hero when he led his hometown Little League to the Williamsport World Championship. Cody was seen as clearly being one of the dominant baseball players of his age group, and then some.

But time passed, and life can be unpredictable, especially in terms of sports development. By the time Cody was fourteen and playing in Pond League games, he was still a fine player, but not as dominant as he had been a few years earlier. He

(continued)

Are Today's Youth Stars Also the Stars of Tomorrow?

even heard some catcalls: *I thought you were the World Series hero. You suck.*

Cody was good enough, however, to play at Eastern Washington University, but then his baseball career came to an end with some shoulder problems. But even by then, Cody knew that his athletic career had seemingly peaked when he was only twelve. "It was hard for me," Webster told the *Seattle Times* in 2001. "I mean, I had a lot of pressure on me throughout my baseball career to produce. It just got to the point when I was seventeen, eighteen, nineteen that I just wasn't as good anymore. It's just a fact."

THE IMPACT OF PREADOLESCENCE: DO KIDS REALLY QUIT SPORTS?

I can't emphasize enough how unpredictable the preteen and teenage years are for children. Yes, we all went through our own adolescent experiences, and I strongly urge you to recall your own adolescence as you watch your child begin to go through it. For most eleven- and twelve-year-olds, middle school is a major rite of passage, not just in terms of sports, but in all phases of life. They begin to find their friends and their passions in life, and they discover the opposite sex, what they like to do in their spare time, and what they don't like. They can become moody, cranky, and at times, downright goofy. Whether it's the adolescent hormones kicking in, or just the experience of being a teenager, you have to bear in mind that lots of priorities in their young lives can seemingly shift overnight.

Their interest in athletics can shift overnight as well. All of a sudden, a twelve-year-old who has never missed a practice or a game might want to know why she has to miss her friend's sleepover birthday party. A conversation like this may follow:

DAUGHTER: *C'mon Mom, all my friends are going to be there, and I don't want to miss it.*

MOM: *But, Samantha, you have a travel soccer practice at 8 a.m. tomorrow!*

DAUGHTER: *But I haven't missed a soccer practice in three months! Why can't I call the coach and tell him I'm sick?*

As a parent, you definitely want your child to socialize with her friends at the sleepover party, but on the other hand, you also know she's made a commitment to be at the travel soccer practice. This is a tough call. Is there a solution? Perhaps you allow Samantha to stay at her friends' home until eleven, when you pick her up so she can go home and get a good night's sleep. Or maybe you can make arrangements to let her stay over with her friends, but warn her that she's going to be very tired the next morning when she goes to practice.

It's the lingering effect of social situations like these that get kids really thinking about how much time and effort they put into their sports. Or, as they become more socially outgoing and active, they begin to realize that more and more of their friends are leaving sports teams and exploring other interests in school. Again, bear in mind that close to three-quarters of all kids who play sports decide to quit by the time they're thirteen. And this growing social pressure is one of the major reasons.

So how do you keep your youngster involved in his sport? Well, that's hard to say. If he was able to develop a passion for his sport when he was younger, this shouldn't be a problem as he goes through middle school. And yes, usually the kids who do well in athletics naturally enjoy the positive feedback and will want to continue their involvement. But a number of youngsters, as the stakes become a little more competitive, will come to the conclusion *on their own* that perhaps continuing in sports is no longer their top priority in life.

To a certain extent, this is what Rachel went through. In elementary and middle school, she played a variety of sports, including basketball, lacrosse, and field hockey. But in high school, she decided on her own to keep playing basketball while devoting a lot of her time to dancing. Kelly and I couldn't be happier for her, because clearly Rachel plays and dances for the right reason: She enjoys doing so!

Again, this is normal. As a parent, if you ask your son whether he plans to try out for the basketball team and you get the sense that he's not really into basketball as much as he used to be, that's fine. But what you should do is ask the following: *John, if you're not to going to play a sport this winter, that's fine with me. But you need to find another after-school activity to keep you busy and involved. What do you have in mind?*

This is an important conversation, because you don't want your child doing nothing after school. Not only is this a waste of time, but it presents lots of opportunities for him to get into trouble or fall in with the wrong crowd. If your youngster has decided that basketball is not in his future, you might also take some time to ask whether he'd like to try another sport, such as swimming, skiing, wrestling, or any other sporting endeavor that he might not have seriously considered before. In other words, don't close any doors—in fact, find some new ones for your child to open.

One other word about kids leaving teams: Long after they get through high school sports, you want them to stay in top physical shape for the rest of their lives. (That's not only a suggestion; it's really become mandatory, especially because so many of our youngsters are facing weight issues these days.) So, even if your child decides to leave organized team sports entirely, make every effort to suggest to her that she find some sort of physical exercise to keep her strong and fit. That could be jogging, hiking, swimming, skateboarding, riding a bike, whatever. But make sure she takes you seriously and make sure she pushes away from the computer or video games and physically works out every day.

SHOULD YOU HOLD YOUR KID BACK A YEAR?

Some parents—either remembering their own teenage years, in which they were late bloomers, or realizing that their youngster might really benefit from an extra year to mature in school—decide to hold their child back a year in school. Depending on the youngster, an additional year of physical and emotional development may be of tremendous help, especially if the child plays sports.

Years ago, this practice of holding a child back or having him repeat a year in school was fairly rare, but now the practice has become a lot more common. Sometimes parents do it when their child is only five or six, before she starts kindergarten or first grade, especially when the child has a birth date that is relatively late in the year. The parents feel they would rather have their child be one of the older kids in the grade than one of the younger ones. This is a personal choice that you'll have to make for your child.

However, some parents hold their child back an extra year in eighth grade, especially if the child is going to move from, say, the local public school to a parochial or private school. The parents feel that the child needs that extra year of eighth grade to help him adapt to new surroundings and new friends in a new school. This holding-back decision is supposed to be for the benefit of the child's overall physical and emotional development, but many times one of the side benefits is that it allows a child to have an extra year to develop as an athlete.

Caution: Does this kind of move automatically guarantee that your child will become one of the better athletes in his class? Of course not. And quite frankly, if the main purpose of holding your child back a year is to get her on the athletic fast track, I strongly urge you to rethink what you are doing. Remember that for any child, being held back a year can bring some unwanted emotional baggage: No kid wants to have to say to his peers that he had to repeat eighth grade when he changed schools. Especially with kids who are twelve or thirteen, be very, very sensitive to their needs and ego if and when you decide to make this kind of move.

If by the time your child is a senior in high school, you honestly feel that she could use an extra year to develop as a promising athlete, you can always opt to send your child for what's known as a "postgraduate" year of high school. This year, routinely referred to as a "P.G." year, gives that seventeen- or eighteen-year-old athlete an extra year of high school studies, which will allow him to fill out, grow, and mature, and even give him a chance to work on his grades before he applies to college. Over the years, this has been a fairly common practice with high school ice hockey and basketball players who want both an extra year to mature physically and an extra year to bolster their grades. But in the last ten years or so, the P.G. year has become part of the academic landscape for other sports as well, including lacrosse and football. If you do want to consider a P.G. year for your youngster, or even the possibility of having her repeat the eighth grade, I strongly urge you to absolutely first have a meeting with your child's school guidance counselor as you weigh your options.

WHAT ABOUT "PLAYING UP"?

Sometimes, kids are asked by the league to play up a level. That is, they play with athletes who are older because they are perceived to be dominant against their same-age peers. I have no problem with this practice, because for the talented kid, it's great to play against better competition at a younger age. But I also say this: In order for this move to have positive results for the child, he has to be good enough to enjoy some level of success at the higher age level.

In other words, if the younger kid is overwhelmed by the step up in competition, then the move will have backfired. Clearly, that's not the purpose of having the kid play up. Most younger kids, given enough time and opportunity, will have some positive experiences in the older group that they can build on. But this is a choice that has to be carefully thought out ahead of time, and then, once the move is made, it has to be closely monitored. It's particularly vital that the coach be very patient with the younger player. This is always a judgment call depending on the individual child, and in my opinion, if there is a real concern as to whether this is a good move for the kid, then I would err on the side of caution, and would prefer that the child not move up.

There's nothing wrong with having that talented youngster play a year every so often with kids her own age anyway. If she's been playing against older kids, it'll be a tremendous confidence boost for her to play against her peers again. Giving kids confidence is always a plus in sports.

Remember: Just because a younger kid has the physical size and ability doesn't necessarily mean that he has the mental makeup to play up. That means being able to deal with frustration and adversity. And again, since every kid is different, there is no general rule.

Key Chapter Takeaways

1. **Be careful about having your child specialize in just one sport when she's still in elementary or middle school. Most kids find that their athletic skills transfer easily from one sport to another.**

2. **When kids are in elementary school, they will often play a couple of sports during the same season. But as they reach middle school, they will find that it will become increasingly difficult to make a commitment to more than one team at the same time.**

3. There is no one, hard-and-fast rule about holding your child back an extra year in school. Such decisions have to be made on an individual basis, and the child's best interests are what count.
4. Hard work alone will only take your child so far in competitive sports. He also needs to be blessed with God-given athletic ability in order to get to the higher levels of sport.

Chapter 8

IMPROVING ONE'S PERFORMANCE: Nutrition, Weight Training, Private Tutors, and Coping with Injuries

Your kids may find it hard to believe, but in the last twenty years, there's been a tremendous upheaval in some of the basic concepts involving sports and one's body. Even when I look back at some of the fundamental assumptions we held about physical conditioning in the 1960s and '70s, I find it's extraordinary how many of these basic beliefs have changed.

For example, once upon a time, kids who aspired to become professional baseball players were told that they should never lift weights. Why? Because, the theory went, the added bulkiness of rippling muscles in their arms and shoulders could seriously jeopardize their throwing motion.

We assumed that major leaguers needed to have long, flowing muscles—not rock-hard biceps and triceps—if they wanted to be successful on the diamond.

Players and coaches thought being a bit overweight in the off-season was okay, too, because you would just lose those extra pounds slowly in the hot sun of spring training. Indeed, for many, many years, ballplayers would often let themselves slip out of shape during the winter months, and then would come to training camp and work very hard to get rid of that spare tire.

It was also accepted that when it came to an athlete's running speed, well, "You can't teach speed—either you're born with it, or you're not." It was also felt that a player's overall athletic coordination could not be improved. That is, if an athlete wasn't quick, or couldn't move well laterally, or couldn't jump too high, well, that was too bad, because there was really nothing you could do about it.

A well-accepted theory about pregame nutrition was that the perfect meal before a big game was a breakfast of steak and eggs and nothing more. Protein—not carbohydrates—was thought to be the key to sustained strength and stamina late in the game.

HOW THE TIMES HAVE CHANGED . . .

Clearly, a lot has changed when it comes to nutrition, strength development, and conditioning. In this chapter, I tell you about some of the latest developments that can help

improve your child's performance. Some of the developments are in direct contrast to many traditional beliefs. For
example, these days all major leaguers know that it makes
no sense to let themselves get out of shape during the winter
months—that it's much healthier and easier to keep up
their conditioning and report to spring training ready to go.

They also know that lifting weights and resistance
training are essential to getting the most out of their bodies. And top athletes now take a very serious interest in
what they eat, not just before a game, but all year. They
know that adding empty calories that taste good, such as
from soda and candy bars, does nothing for their athletic
framework and strength, so they try hard to read the nutrition labels, and they train themselves to reach for an
apple or a banana instead of a cupcake or a doughnut.

This is not to say that, as a parent, you should never
let your youngster enjoy pizza, soda, candy, or other fun
foods that kids like. To never allow your child to enjoy
himself would be foolish. Besides, we all know that kids today can be very finicky or picky eaters, and that they are
immediately drawn to the fattening, processed foods. So
instead of just always saying no, no, no, try a more positive
approach. While they're still in elementary school, try to
educate your young athletes about sampling some of the
healthier foods if they want to continue to grow strong
and be healthy. You don't have to lecture them, but make
it clear every so often that all of the top athletes these days
watch what they eat carefully, whether it be Tiger Woods

or Derek Jeter or Peyton Manning. They all do, because they have learned that if they don't take care of their bodies, their bodies won't take care of them.

Looking back, my mom's advice was right on target. She always urged three good meals a day, including vegetables. Snacks were okay in moderation. In short, Mom believed that good nutrition for all activities started with good ol' common sense.

Nutrition, as you know, is no small concern these days. Unfortunately, in the last decade or so, childhood obesity has become a major worry to health care professionals everywhere. By most accounts, kids are simply eating too much (e.g., *Do you want me to supersize that meal?* and *Do you want the forty-eight- or sixty-four-ounce soda?*), but our children are working out and exercising less and less. And don't think for a second this applies only to the kids who aren't athletically inclined. Even kids who do play sports are spending more and more time eating during their downtime, and also just sitting in front of their computers or televisions. Besides, what happens to our young athletes when they do stop competing in sports? They may stop burning all those calories on the field, but their eating habits stay the same, and in some cases, they become worse. That's why so many doctors are very, very worried.

You can go to any number of resources and Web sites to check on healthy eating programs for your child. And if your child does have a particular issue with healthy eating, by all means be sure to check with your pediatrician. All pediatricians these days are well versed in food and related health issues, and if not, they will certainly know how to direct you to other resources. While you're talking with your pediatrician, you can also inquire about pregame and during-game nutrition. Don't be surprised if he or she suggests carbohydrates for pregames, such as pancakes, toast, and peanut butter sandwiches. For quick snacks during the games, try granola or energy bars. They offer a good combination of carbohydrates and protein, and are relatively low in fat content. Just be sure to check the nutrition label on the energy bars. Try to find bars that contain two hundred calories or fewer.

Above all, use common sense. Make sure your youngster has a chance to digest her food before she runs out on the field or onto the court. If it's hot, make sure your child has plenty of cool liquids to drink during the game. If it's cold, make sure he has hot chocolate, ready and available. And when the game is over, make sure that your young player doesn't chug down huge amounts of food and drink as soon as she comes off the field.

PLYOMETRICS FOR BUILDING AGILITY, QUICKNESS, AND BALANCE

In recent years, the growing science of plyometrics has been eagerly adopted by a number of pro and college teams in a variety of sports. Plyometric exercise is a relatively new term,

Obesity Epidemic

According to the Centers for Disease Control and Prevention, obesity among American children has reached an alarming level. Thirteen percent of all Caucasian boys are significantly overweight, 20.5 percent of all African-American teenage boys are obese, and 27.5 percent of teenage boys of Mexican descent are obese.

In sum, more than 15 percent of American kids are obese, which is defined as having a body mass index higher than the ninety-fifth percentile for their age and gender. In contrast, in the 1960s, less than 4 percent of children fit that profile.

Why is this happening? A recent National Association for Sports & Physical Education (NASPE) survey found that virtually every state has reduced its phys ed requirements over the last thirty years. Specifically:

Only seven states require elementary schools to have certified phys ed instructors, meaning that classroom teachers are often responsible for teaching gym class.

Only about 26 percent of U.S. high school students get daily physical education. Illinois is the only state that still requires it.

Forty percent of high school students are not enrolled in gym class of any kind. For high school seniors the number is a staggering 75 percent.

In fact, when our foundation recently went on a twenty-five-state tour awarding grants to many schools, our instructors were often asked to run gym class for that day because the schools were not staffed for it.

so don't be put off if you haven't heard of it before. But it's now the rare pro or college team that doesn't incorporate it, or urge its athletes to do plyometric exercises.

Plyometrics focus on a series of short-burst exercises that are designed to help any athlete develop quickness, jumping ability, lateral movement, and forward and backward movement. The exercises are meant to be repetitive, but certainly won't tire any youngster out. In fact, most kids find them to be quite enjoyable. A typical plyometric session doesn't last more than fifteen to twenty minutes a day, and can easily be incorporated into any youngster's daily practice routine.

Better yet, because there are so many different types of plyometric exercises, a young athlete can find the right series of plyometrics to meet his individual needs. That is, some kids want to work on their balance, others want to develop their quickness or jumping ability. Whatever the concern is, there are plyometric exercises that can help your child. Many kids start doing plyometrics when they are still in elementary school, and they can continue with their exercises right through high school and beyond.

Here's a small sampling of some typical plyometric exercises (there are plenty more to choose from):

Jumping Rope: Most kids know how to jump rope, and enjoy it. The key in the plyometric version is that when your child jumps over the rope, she lands on the balls of her feet—all the time. That's important.

If your youngster jumps rope for, say, five to seven minutes at a time—and he's able to land and jump from the balls of his feet while doing this—over a few weeks' time, he will begin to build a much stronger feeling of foot quickness. No matter what sport skill he wishes to develop, whether it's getting a good jump on a ball in the outfield, trying to outsprint an opponent to a soccer ball, or trying to quicken his lateral movement in basketball, plyometrics is a wonderful way to accomplish that.

Box Run: Find a small but sturdy wooden box that's no more than ten inches high. Have your child start with her right foot on top of the box, and the other foot on the floor. Then, while she is moving her feet quickly, have her jump up, switching her feet back and forth from the top of the box to the floor. Have your child repeat this movement twenty times, let her rest for a moment or two, and then have her do it again and again. This is an excellent training aid to increase sprint speed, agility, and balance.

Box Jump: Have your athlete stand with both feet on that same wooden box. (Or if the box isn't strong enough, you can use a low outside step.) Make sure the youngster's toes are on the edge of the box, but with her heels hanging off the edge. Have her jump off the box and then back onto it as quickly as possible. Let her do this fifteen times in a row, always trying to land her toes on the edge of the box when jumping back onto it. Have her do three sets of fifteen jumps. This box jump exercise is particularly good conditioning for improving one's vertical leaping ability.

Again, these are only a few samples of some of the better-known and easier-to-do plyometric exercises. Kids as young as seven or eight can start doing these drills, and stay with them right through their middle school and high school years. For more information, there are lots of books on the subject. Be sure to check out your local library for more on plyometrics.

SPEED TRAINING FOR KIDS?

According to top speed experts, like Dr. Bob Clark (www .speedscience.com), who has extensively studied the science of running sprints, very few kids are ever taught how to run properly. That is, when our children first go out and start running around, they just run instinctively in whatever style comes naturally to them. It isn't until they match up against their peers in elementary or middle school that they begin to see that there are distinct differences in style.

According to Dr. Clark, who graduated from Stanford University Medical School and first became intrigued with the science of speed running when his football-playing son wanted to improve his sprint times, the key is for a youngster to learn how to develop a quick start by pushing off and running on the balls of his feet. If you take a moment to watch kids run in a game, you'll see that most of them run with their heel landing first before they push off on their toes. To be sure, there are lots of other important mechanics to running fast, such as knowing the proper way to pump one's arms and also how to tilt (or not tilt) one's body forward, but the bottom line is that athletic kids can be trained to run faster.

Does this mean that your twelve-year-old with average speed can be trained and taught to become a top Olympic sprinter? Most likely not. But through proper training and evaluation, she can eventually learn how to perform to the best of her ability. For most kids, that means perhaps shaving a few tenths of a second off their forty- or sixty-yard dash. For example, for a high school or college baseball player to be considered a good prospect, running a 6.8 in the sixty-yard dash is considered much better than a 7.1. Or for a football player, being clocked at a 4.6 in the forty is a marked improvement from running a 4.8 or 4.9. Again, the concept of being able to improve one's speed is a relatively new development when it comes to performance enhancement breakthroughs in sports.

WEIGHT TRAINING AT YOUNGER AGES?

While it's now fairly well accepted that kids—even kids as young as ten or eleven—can start weight training, this is one area in which parents have to be careful and constantly monitor their youngster's involvement.

Before enrolling your child in any kind of weight-training program, discuss it with your pediatrician or family physician. Let the doctor know that your child is thinking of doing some weight training, and that your youngster is probably going to lift weights at least three times a week. Sometimes, upon hearing this, the physician might recommend a particular trainer the doctor knows and trusts. Or, on the other hand, the doctor may question why your child wants to do this. Either way, make sure you get the physician's professional blessing, because there are some inherent worries about weight training. For example, the growth plates in your child's arms and legs might be detrimentally affected by lifting too many weights. That could cause serious complications for your youngster as he continues to grow through adolescence.

However, assuming that your family doctor does clear your child for weight training, be sure to find an athletic trainer who is well qualified. Be very wary of the high school kid who says, *Sure, I'll be glad to teach your son about weight lifting.* That's to be avoided at all costs! You need to find a certified and experienced trainer who will meet with you and your child to go over exactly what the training regimen involves, and how it can help your youngster. You should also be certain to get some background on the trainer and his or her credentials.

Finally, during this very important meeting with the trainer, be sure to ask how soon your child will see any tangible results. This is key, because most kids think that they're going to see major improvements within a week or so. They fully expect that their pipe-cleaner arms are going to be transformed into massive biceps by the end of the month. In fact, one of the major reasons kids end up quitting is precisely this: They aren't seeing the kinds of results they wanted. Remember, our children are growing up in an instant-gratification world, and they expect to see positive results immediately, if not sooner.

Keep reminding your child to be patient—that just because he doesn't see the results of his weight training right away, it doesn't mean that he isn't making progress and getting stronger. Most weight-training programs have the participants keep active charts, so that they can map their advancement week after week. That should be enough strong evidence for kids to see that they are getting stronger, and that if they continue with the program, they will see their bodies begin to respond to their efforts. But this all takes time.

PERFORMANCE-ENHANCING SUBSTANCES: STEROIDS, CREATINE, ANDRO, EPHEDRA, HGH

Unfortunately, as you know, some athletes don't want to spend the time necessary to improve their body strength in a healthy and natural way through hard work. These athletes cheat by turning to illegal performance-enhancing substances, like steroids, to help them improve their game. Steroids, of course, affect an athlete's body in all sorts of terrible ways. I never used any steroids in my baseball career, and I sure don't want my kids or anyone else's to use them, either. But in addition to steroids, there are other substances that sports parents should be aware of.

I'll start with creatine. This product, which is a heavily concentrated dose of protein, is relatively new on the market, and in truth, medical scientists do not yet know its long-range impact on the human body. The question parents have to ask is: If the medical community doesn't know creatine's long-term consequences, do I really want my child to use this stuff?

There is solid evidence that creatine can cause severe dehydration and cramping in athletes who use it, and the NCAA has strongly urged its athletes not to use it. But because creatine is considered a dietary supplement (and thus not regulated by the FDA), it is sold legally in health food and nutrition stores everywhere. Problem is, most kids (and parents) automatically assume that if a product is sold legally in a store, then it must be safe to ingest. Again, as a parent, just remember that no one knows for sure whether creatine is safe.

Androstenedione, or andro, as it is more commonly known, first came into America's mainstream consciousness thanks to Mark McGwire of the St. Louis Cardinals. The former home run slugger openly admitted using andro during his record-breaking year in 1998. At that time, andro was not banned from baseball, and so McGwire was within his rights to do that.

But the year after McGwire broke the single-season home run record, he stopped using andro. Mark gave no real reason as to why he stopped. But there has been an avalanche of newspaper and magazine articles since 1998 about how dangerous andro can be. It's a medical precursor to steroids, so users should be very concerned about their long-range health. A year or two after McGwire stopped using it, major league baseball joined all the rest of the professional sports leagues by officially banning andro as well.

Ephedra is another potentially dangerous substance parents should know about. Ephedra has long been known to pro and college athletes as a way to lose weight in a hurry by speeding up the body's metabolism. Just a couple of years ago, Orioles pitcher Steve Bechler collapsed and died in spring training. Steve had been using a product with ephedra in it and there is speculation that this contributed to his death. Again, be sure to caution your athlete about the lethal dangers of ephedra.

Finally, human growth hormone (HGH) is another performance enhancer that increases the user's size and stature. Originally designed only for children who are severely undersized, HGH has found its way into the sports world. Athletes in their prime have found that HGH helps them keep their muscle mass for a longer time, and HGH has become a well-known performance enhancer.

Fortunately, HGH is not very popular with kids. For starters, it is very expensive, has to be administered with a needle injection every day, doesn't always pay off with the results that the youngster wanted (the average change in height is only one to two inches), and has to be prescribed by a physician who has to monitor its results over time. If, as a parent, you are truly concerned about your child's

size, then you can certainly check with your family physician about HGH. Just be careful not to expect any mira-
cles to happen overnight.

Overall, as a parent who wants to make sure that your
youngster stays healthy not only during her playing career
but long afterward, it's squarely upon your shoulders to
monitor what your child is ingesting. If you simply look the
other way, or aren't concerned when your child puts on
twenty-five pounds of pure muscle over the course of a few
weeks, then you're just not being fair to your kid. And please
don't think this issue is a minor one, or one that may not be
in your neighborhood. Recent statistical surveys show that
steroid use, as well as use of other performance enhancers,
has risen dramatically in the last decade all over the country.

WHAT ABOUT HIRING A PRIVATE COACH?

One of the more recent developments with youth sports is
the advent of private coaching. The private coach is usually an adult who has specialized expertise in that sport,
and he or she is paid anywhere from $50 to $100 an hour
for tutoring a young athlete. Usually, the sessions are individualized, that is, one-to-one sessions between the athlete
and the coach. But sometimes, there might be three or
four kids in the same session.

Personally, I don't have a problem with hiring a private
coach. In many regards, the process is parallel to a parent
hiring an academic tutor for their youngster if the child is

Steroid Use on the Increase

There have been reports from all over the country that steroid use is on the rise with both teenage boys and girls. According to a University of Michigan study that was reported in *Newsweek*, more than 300,000 students between eighth and twelfth grade used steroids in 2003. The study goes on to say that at least a third of those using steroids were girls, who were eager to improve their body image.

In addition, the Michigan study also found there was a significant drop in the number of high school seniors who consider using steroids to be "of great risk" to their personal health. In effect, kids today are less and less concerned about the long-range impact of steroids on their bodies, even though there is overwhelming evidence that steroids are extremely dangerous.

Newsweek also reported that those youngsters who use steroids were surprised at how little notice their parents and coaches took of the changes that were quickly taking shape before their eyes. That is, either the parents and coaches just weren't paying attention or they didn't want to.

Telltale Signs of Steroid Use

- Increased acne, especially on the back
- Significant boost in size, weight, and muscular development
- Extreme moodiness and outbursts of anger, even paranoia

struggling in, say, math class or English class. Put it this way: If your child were having a hard time with geometry, wouldn't you hire a tutor to help him over the hurdle? I think the same thinking applies to private coaches. If your son or daughter is having a tough time learning how to shoot free throws, how to skate backward in hockey, or how to throw strikes, it makes sense to find a private coach who can help. In some individualized sports, the concept of personal coaches has been around a long time. Golf pros, tennis instructors, swim instructors, ski coaches, and gymnastic coaches have been accepted for years by parents who want their children to learn how to develop the right playing techniques at a relatively young age. In effect, this concept has just spread from the individual sports world to that of team sports.

Private coaching can be very effective, especially if you, as a parent, can't provide the kind of specialized training that your child wants or needs. For example, let's say your eleven-year-old needs some expert training on how to dribble a soccer ball with either foot. Problem is, you never played soccer as a kid and you don't have much expertise to offer to your child. There's nothing wrong with hiring a skilled soccer coach to help teach and work with your child to develop this important skill. (Of course, hiring private coaches can be expensive, so clearly you have to make sure it fits into your family budget.)

Additionally, and I know I have mentioned this before, don't force more instruction on your child. Make sure this is something that the child wants, or you will be just wasting time and money and taking the joy of the sport away from your child.

VIDEOTAPING YOUR ATHLETE AS AN INSTRUCTIONAL TOOL

These days, it seems that every parent who has a child playing a sport always brings a video camera to record the kid's performance in the games. That's fine; if nothing else, the videotape serves as a keepsake for the youngster to look at when he gets older. The video serves as a kind of modern-day scrapbook for the young athlete.

But what's always been curious to me about all those parents who videotape their kids is that I'm not sure they realize how that video can really aid their kids in terms of actual instruction and in improving their play. That is, if you take the time and learn the best ways to videotape some of your child's performances, then you can have the tape serve two purposes: one, as a family scrapbook that the youngster can watch and review, over and over again; and two, as a truly invaluable instructional tool.

For well over thirty years, sports psychologists have urged serious athletes to learn how to "visualize" their performances in upcoming games. The process of visualization works on the theory that your brain subconsciously controls your body's neuromuscular system, and if you can "preprogram" your key neuromuscular connections to perform in just the right way, then you can, in effect, program your athletic body to always perform at a high level.

Visualization techniques have been used around the world, and for the most part, top athletes find that this approach works for them, although in varying degrees. But more recently, in a study conducted by the Association for the Advancement for Applied Sports Psychology, it was discovered that top athletes can also benefit greatly from watching videotaped performances of themselves in action. This video instruction works very well when athletes have a chance to observe themselves performing at an optimum level. Indeed, many top sports psychologists (as well as myself) suggest that struggling athletes watch video "highlight" reels of themselves, so that the visual imagery sinks in, over and over again. The key in the process is that the videotape show those plays when the athlete has been performing well (e.g., making all of her shots from the court, having a perfect drive off the tee, etc.). Only by watching videotape of top performances can an athlete begin to find that "groove" that he's looking for.

Pro and college athletes will often spend several hours in the tape room, first looking at one of their poor performances, and then contrasting that tape with their personal highlight reel. Invariably, the athlete will find some key difference in her technique or approach that makes a big difference in her performance. This difference may be very subtle to the outsider, but it'll be very apparent to the individual athlete who can compare his style in both tapes.

SO HOW DOES "VIDEO VISUALIZATION" WORK?

Some basic steps to follow: First, of course, be very familiar with your camera. Learn how to zoom in for close action. Realize that if you have to shoot directly into the sunlight, chances are you won't get much action on the tape because the sun will blot it out. Naturally, your best bet is to shoot the action with the sun at your back.

Then there's the problem of trying to find the right spot on the field to tape your child. If your son or daughter is playing on a field that is surrounded by a chain-link fence, you'll have to experiment to find the best way to shoot either through, or over, the mesh of the fence. (My personal preference is to get the lens of the camera as close as possible to the holes in the fence.)

If the weather is very cold or wet, you'll have other problems. You have to make certain that the lens doesn't get wet or covered with condensation. Be prepared to bring along whatever essentials you need to make sure you're ready to take care of the videotaping process. Naturally, a lot of this is common sense. But to do the job right takes some planning—and some experimenting—to make certain you know the best way to tape the games and your son or daughter in action.

The sport your youngster plays will determine how difficult it is, or isn't, to tape her in action. Baseball and softball, of course, are relatively simple. Videotaping a pitcher from behind the backstop, or shooting tape of a hitter from the side of the backstop, is easy. But trying to tape a youngster playing in a soccer or field hockey game is most challenging because, quite frankly, you never know when the ball is going to his part of the field. You have to learn how to anticipate when the action is going to involve your child, and then be ready to start the tape when it appears that the ball is going to her.

Then—and most important—you have to discipline yourself not to jostle the camera when you're taping the action. This, of course, tends to be somewhat nerve-racking, to stay focused on the tape when everybody around you is cheering. Many times, when I have taped my children playing sports—which means looking through a small eyepiece on the camera—I really don't get a chance to see and enjoy the action while it's actually happening. I have to wait to watch the videotape later in the day, but when I do, I can sit down and share the joy with my kids.

WHEN YOUR YOUNGSTER VIEWS THE TAPE

As a sports parent, this is where you have to be a little patient. When your child first sits down to watch the videotape, allow him the pleasure of watching it several times. With the first few times, realize that he's going to watch the tape as he would watch a new movie or television show. That is, he's watching simply for fun and pleasure—not so much to analyze his actions.

But once your child has enjoyed the tape a few times, then you might want to invite her—and this is strictly an invite, never a demand—to sit down and go over her individual plays with you. Just as a football coach will watch videotape of previous games, you can go over the various highlights of your child's performance. Note: To keep your youngster absorbed, go over the high points of her performance first. Heap lots of praise on the actions or plays that she did well.

Note again: This is not the time to focus on those parts of the game where your child made mistakes and played poorly. Remember, the purpose of the videotape session is to recognize and reinforce those positive parts of his game. The idea here is to take visualization to a higher level in his mind's eye. That is, if he can literally see himself doing well on the video—and he can watch the video over and over again—then he is, in effect, programming his mind, muscles, and nervous system to be consistent in his athletic actions.

It will come as no surprise that professional baseball players are huge devotees of this form of video visualization. They will look at highlight reels of themselves hitting well, or pitching well. The same philosophy is used by professional and college basketball players, who want to see their form when they shoot a jump shot or a free throw. This technique is commonly used by just about all professional athletes these days, who want to reinforce consistent athletic patterns in their performances.

Coaches, instructors, and athletes have all found that there's no better way to communicate technique improvements than by having athletes view themselves on tape. Most parents take video of their kids' games and then put the tapes away in some sort of video scrapbook. But there's nothing wrong at all with letting your child become familiar and comfortable with the use of videotape to strengthen and improve his or her game.

THE "THIRD PARTY" INTERMEDIARY

In addition to the actual physical training, I have noticed that there's an added benefit to having another adult work with a child. I call this the "third-party approach" to coaching kids. The truth is that, sometimes, parents have a difficult time communicating with their youngster about their sport. Whatever the psychological reason or barrier may be, occasionally some real friction can occur between the parent and the child:

> DAD: C'mon, try swinging the bat this way. . . .
> JAKE: No, Dad, I want to do it my way . . .
> DAD: But, Jake, trust me . . . this is the right way to do it!
> JAKE: I don't care! Just leave me alone . . .

These kinds of flare-ups, which can happen between parent and child, rarely occur when a private coach is working with the child. In much the same way a child is less likely to be resistant to being tutored by her teacher in school, she is less likely to be resistant when a private coach asks her to try something different in her approach. There's just something about a third party (e.g., a coach or a teacher) that allows the kid to feel less pressure and also to be more attentive about the instruction or tutoring.

I have seen this dynamic take place between parent and athlete many times, and as a parent myself, I found it out firsthand. I was working with Ryan on an aspect of his hitting, and he was very reluctant to listen to me because it ran counter to what his coach was telling him. I suggested that I might have a little more baseball knowledge than his coach, but it just didn't matter! If you find that your child is not eager to work with you, you might want to solicit the aid of another coach. That could be another adult who serves as the coach or assistant coach on your child's team, or it could be someone you hire as a private coach for your son or daughter. Again, it can make a big difference:

> COACH: Jake, I've been watching you swing the bat the last few games . . . and if it's okay with you, I'd like to see you try a little different approach in the batter's box . . .
>
> JAKE: Um . . . okay. What do you want me to do?

Again, it's hard to explain why this kind of "third-party approach" works so well, but the youngster will at least respond and try what the coach is suggesting. And if the youngster does, in fact, find some real improvement, don't be surprised if he comes back to you a day or two later and wants to show you what he has learned from the coach.

BE CAREFUL OF ACCIDENTALLY PLACING TOO MUCH PRESSURE ON YOUR KID

One of the subtle psychological concerns of having your son or daughter play the same sport that you did as a kid is that, quite accidentally, you might add extra pressure on your child. Especially if you reached a certain level of success in that sport, your child may instinctively feel that he or she has to not only live up to your level of success but even try to surpass it.

That's a difficult proposition to be sure. For example, when Ryan plays in baseball tournaments, lots of fans will immediately be drawn to see Cal Ripken's son. Rightly or wrongly, Ryan will become the focus of a lot of attention. I had a little bit of that when I was a kid, since my dad was a minor league manager, but not like what Ryan has to cope with. I try to listen to him whenever he wants to talk about this unnecessary attention, and I try to pump him up. But more important, I remind him of all the times I struggled with the game, the errors I made, the hundreds of strike-outs, and so on. It's important that all of us parents let our kids know that we struggled with the sports we played when we were kids, so that our kids don't think that we expect them to be perfect in their sports.

Although that may seem obvious to us, I think it bears repeating. Be sure to let your son or daughter know that you had lots of tough days on the athletic field as well. In short, take some of the pressure off your child.

KIDS COPING WITH INJURIES

Any pro athlete will tell you that there is nothing more frustrating than being injured. And for kids, it's even tougher. Having to stand or sit on the sidelines and watch one's friends and teammates play in games or practice is very tough. It's just as tough on you because there's not much you can do to help speed the healing process. If your child sprains an ankle or gets a shoulder banged up or whatever the injury may be, and the doctor gives explicit orders to not play for at least two or three weeks or even longer, you have to make sure your youngster doesn't come back to play too soon.

For a kid, two to three weeks may seem like a life sentence. But if nothing else, teach your athlete to always listen to the doctor. After all, if the child comes back and plays too soon—and reinjures herself—then the youngster might be out for a much longer period of time. Tell her that she is running that risk.

Although I was pretty healthy during my big-league

career, I suffered through a variety of injuries in high school and in the minors, and I missed games. Dad always made sure that I understood the risks of trying to return to the playing field prematurely.

All of this may seem like common sense. But I also know that it's sometimes the parents who are eager to see their child return, and that they willingly give their approval when perhaps they shouldn't. For example, a parent on the sidelines might see his or her youngster get her head accidentally banged a bit on a play. She falls to the ground and is momentarily dazed, play is stopped, and then the child comes off the field. The coach keeps her out of the game for the rest of the first half, but then, in the second half, the coach asks her parents if she can play again, and Mom and Dad say, sure, she seems fine. But head injuries and concussions can be very hard to diagnose, and even though the child seems to be okay, it is a bit of a risk to send her back into the game. For example, what happens if she bangs her head again in the second half? These are the kinds of situations when Mom and Dad have to act as adults first and sports parents second.

Fortunately, many times at kids' sporting events there will be a nurse or physician in attendance who has a child playing in the game. If a potentially dangerous injury does occur, it's always wise to solicit professional advice from that nurse or doctor about the child's health and welfare before allowing him to resume playing. If a medical professional is not in attendance, then use common sense, and always err on the side of caution. *Remember: There's never any reason to risk a child's long-term health.*

Finally, understand that every sport comes with a certain amount of risk. Bumps and bruises are part of any sporting endeavor. The good news is that there have been tremendous strides in sports medicine in recent years, and athletes heal and bounce back from injuries quickly. I can recall when, not too many years ago, if an athlete suffered a knee injury, it would mean major surgery, and the athlete would definitely be out for the rest of the year and maybe longer. But these days, orthopedic surgeons can perform arthroscopic surgery on knees and shoulders, and players can come back to full strength in just a matter of weeks.

Just keep in mind that injuries do occasionally happen. It's up to you to make sure your child doesn't take the risk of turning a relatively minor injury into a much more serious one by coming back to play too soon.

Key Chapter Takeaways

1. **Educate your child about nutrition, not only what her body needs to keep her energy high, but also what substances and supplements can be potentially dangerous.**

2. **Knowledge and understanding of weight training, physical fitness, and plyometric training have**

advanced rapidly in the last ten or fifteen years. Take the time to educate yourself about the new approaches in these fields when it comes to kids and sports.

3. Listen to your child if he complains about a nagging injury. Most kids bounce back fairly quickly from routine bumps and bruises, so if they complain about a pain that won't go away, pay attention and get some medical help right away.

A FINAL WORD

I do hope that this book has helped in some way. Yes, I used to be a major league baseball player. That was my job, and it was very important to me. But these days my wife Kelly and I focus a great deal of our lives on being parents, and there is nothing more important to us in this world than our kids, Rachel and Ryan. I'm sure you feel the same way about your children.

As adults, we're well aware that time passes very quickly. While our kids bask in the spontaneous glory of their childhood—where time never seems to be a major concern—we know that our children will be kids only for a few precious years.

That same reality applies to their involvement in youth sports. If they don't have a chance to go out and enjoy their years in athletics, well, then the seasons pass by quickly and those experiences are gone. It's up to all of us as sports parents to keep our perspectives and our priorities in order. That means we should be supportive of our children, but never to the point where we are pushing our own sports dreams onto theirs. *Youth sports are supposed to center on our children, not on us.*

One bit of personal advice. Be sure to get lots of photos and videotape of your kids in action. It may seem silly to them when you're out there taping, but trust me, you and your entire family will come to cherish those photos and videotapes as your children go on to high school, college, and their own families. Our kids are kids only once.

I learned about sports and competition primarily from my dad, although certainly Mom was always there to give me lots of encouragement and support. Dad was often away with his baseball career and didn't see many of my youth games, yet somehow he always found the time to say just the right words, to give me that pat on the back, and to give me the space I needed when things weren't going the right way for me on the ball field. He was also there to share in my joy when my dreams came true.

I didn't know it at the time, of course, but clearly those sports-parenting lessons from Dad are the same lessons I have tried to follow with my own children. Most of those lessons are based upon simple fundamentals: patience, praise, practice, and so on. But perhaps the most important lesson I learned from Dad was to sit back and stay out of the way.

In short, let the kids play the games. We had our childhood. It's our kids' childhood now. It's time for us to simply let them go out and watch them enjoy themselves.

—Cal Ripken, Jr.
Fall 2005

Index

*Note: Page numbers in **bold** indicate chapters.*

Index

Index

Index

REGISTER TODAY FOR RIPKEN BASEBALL'S ONLINE SPORTS-PARENTING NEWSLETTER!

FREE TO REGISTER!

To coincide with the release of *Parenting Young Athletes the Ripken Way*, Ripken Baseball will introduce a sports-parenting newsletter in April 2006. This online resource will be filled with essential tips for parents as they guide their children through youth sports.

Sent monthly, the e-newsletter will include excerpts from some of the most noted figures in youth sports, sports psychology, health, coaching, nutrition, and sports medicine. In addition, sports parents from all over the United States who have a passion for the development of youth sports will be contributing their ideas and comments to the e-newsletter.

Initial topics will include:

- *Parenting Young Athletes the Ripken Way* book excerpts
- Tips of the month
- Rising issues within the world of youth sports
- Giving the game back to the kids
- Cal's journal

And much more!

Register today by logging on to
www.ripkenbaseball.com/sportsparenting